CARLY HOLMES lives and writes in a small village on the banks of the river Teifi in west Wales. She is the author of the novels *The Scrapbook*, which was shortlisted for the International Rubery Book Award, and *Crow Face, Doll Face*. Her short story collection, *Figurehead*, was published by Tartarus Press in limited-edition hardback and reprinted in paperback by Parthian Books. She has had numerous stories published in journals and anthologies.

Encouraged by his grandfather, GUY MANNING has been drawing birds since he was a small boy. He has been a window cleaner, barman, kitchen porter, lecturer and teacher, whilst having many exhibitions near and far. He became a full-time artist in 2018 when he and his wife – author Eloise Williams – opened The Art Room in Tenby: a slightly scruffy studio shop where Guy paints and sells his oil paintings and encourages future generations of artists.

LOVE LETTERS ON THE RIVER

Love Letters on the river
CARLY HOLMES

ILLUSTRATED BY
GUY MANNING

PARTHIAN

Parthian
The Old Surgery
Napier Street
Cardigan
SA43 1ED

www.parthianbooks.com

© Carly Holmes, 2025
illustrations © Guy Manning
All Rights Reserved

ISBN: 978-1-917140-26-3

Designed by Olwen Fowler
Printed and bound by 4Edge

The publisher acknowledges the
support of the Books Council of Wales

British Library Cataloguing in Publication Data

A cataloguing record for this book
is available from the British Library

This book is sold subject to the condition that it shall
not by way of trade or otherwise be circulated without
the publisher's prior consent in any form of binding
or cover other than that in which it is published.

For my husband, Si.
With my love, always

Contents

9	**Foreword**
16	**BEYOND THE GARDEN WALL**
18	Mating Cuckoos by Foxhill Farm
22	Juvenile Osprey on the Teifi Estuary
39	Skydancing Ravens at Cwm Gwaun
42	Nightjar at Cross Inn Forest
47	Bittern at the Teifi Marshes
52	**IN THE GARDEN**
54	Runty
61	Tapdancing Tawny Owls
64	Steak Dinner for Four
72	Des Res
83	Pumpkin Eyes
90	The Bereft Sparrowhawk
93	Dawn Chorus
96	**BEYOND THE GARDEN WALL**
98	Winter Barn Owl over the Teifi Marshes
104	Hobbies at Cors Caron
110	Swifts at the Watch House
114	Racing Swans on the Teifi
121	Murmurating Starlings over the Teifi Marshes
125	Crossbills at Pantmaenog Forest
134	**Afterword**

Foreword

This book isn't intended as an expert's observations on the natural world, for I'm no expert when it comes to wildlife. Neither do I have a detached and scientific approach to nature. I unabashedly love the wild creatures I encounter and I gave up feeling embarrassed or ashamed for that love, that lack of detachment, a long time ago.

I try not to anthropomorphise animals except in a light-hearted, humorous way, one that doesn't harm them or deny their essential wildness. But I also accept that I will slip at times, because I'm human and so my point of reference, the filters I apply to the world around me, are necessarily human, too. Besides, I don't think anthropomorphising animals needs to be an inherently negative thing, for surely it's through seeking connections and similarities that we form bonds of affection and a desire to cherish, and god knows the natural world needs to be cherished.

I read nature books to educate myself, and nature books that focus on animals I particularly love – Mark Cocker's *Crow Country*, for example – and I also read the newer breed of nature memoir, the kind of book that turns the natural world into a jumping-off point for humans to explore themselves: their musings on grief or divorce, becoming a parent or losing a parent. Nature as guide, as healer, as provider. A natural world that only seems to exist in relation to us, its value lying in the service it provides.

I don't view nature as a frame for humans and their preoccupations. It isn't there as a backdrop for the next Instagram post or the perfect saleable photograph. It's not a theme park, to be sampled on a day out. I don't chase rare birds around the county or country simply to tick them off a list – the pleasure seemingly lying in the achievement of the sighting and not the sighting itself – and I don't have expensive equipment to record this or that creature's existence before moving briskly on to the next thing. Seeing a bittern for the first time at my local wildlife reserve is of course going to be more of a thrill than seeing the long-tailed tits on the feeders in the garden for the twentieth time that day, but the pleasure I take from sitting quietly and watching those pretty little birds with their showgirl outfits and perfect pink eye shadow is just as profound.

It makes me happy to stand in the street outside my home and watch the house sparrows hanging rudely out of the entrance to the swift box I *didn't* actually put up just for them. Lording it over their rivals, yelling to anyone who'll listen that their spacious new pad – thank you very much, by the way – is so much better than some dank and cobwebby crevice tucked behind a drainpipe. They've raised three broods this year and fledged them all successfully. I'd love to know that box is being used to protect and shelter a new generation of swifts, but to see it protect and shelter any bird raising a family is a joy.

For me, the natural world exists alongside us, sometimes entwined with us, and often despite us. It fills me with a sense of wonder and awe to see such busyness and life all around me, all the time. The unruly patch of nettles at the end of the garden providing food for the caterpillars; the caterpillars providing an essential meal for the blackbirds; the sparrowhawk plunging out of the sun to take one of the blackbirds and then flying fast and low over the garden fences, trailing alarm calls and glossy jet feathers. I am nowhere in these scenes of survival and death.

My existence, except as provider of sunflower hearts and peanuts, is without importance.

And yet by providing this food, and shelters for these creatures, I have inserted myself into the periphery of their lives in ways that are both positive and negative. If the thrushes hadn't been enticed into my garden by the mealworms I put out, then the sparrowhawk wouldn't have taken one of them. If I hadn't put the mealworms out during the summer drought when the top layers of the earth hardened to rock and the worms sank to deeper, moister layers, then the thrush and its chicks may well have starved to death. I feel the push and pull of my meddling constantly, my impulse to care and keep them safe versus my equally keen impulse to leave them be as wild as possible. To love them as best I can, in ways that will only do good.

My grandfather on my father's side was an enigma. Of Roma descent – the surname Holmes, according to family lore, he apparently adopted after seeing it on a gravestone – he was a farm labourer who worked and lived in the rural landscape around Canterbury. He was a formidable and scary figure when I was a small child, for he didn't like children and was inclined to let that dislike show. Remembering him now, I wish I'd known him better or known him when I became an adult. I think we would have got along well, or as well as he was capable of getting along with his fellow humans.

He rose with the dawn and went for long walks with Jenny, the terrier he adored, checking on the birds' nests along his meandering route through fields, orchards, and woodland. He knew where the wrens and the kestrels nested and where the weasels had their dens. Sometimes he stayed out for several hours, particularly when there were visitors to the house. He loved wild creatures and didn't have much patience for humans. I wonder whether that sense of love and fascination we share was passed down to me via the essential, inescapable tangle of genes, or whether it was imprinted on my father as a way of life and then in turn onto me.

I was born on Jersey – the island my mother and the maternal line of the family are from – and spent the majority of my young childhood on a council estate near Southampton before my family moved to west Wales when I was eleven. My memories of those early formative years are fragmented: some things are still sharply in focus while others are wavering and indistinct. I remember, as the only two vegetarians at our school as well as being in receipt of free school meals, that my brother and I had to wait separately from the mainstream lunch queue. Every day we were fed last, cursorily handed a plate heaped high with grated cheddar and then dismissed. Waved away to add boiled vegetables from the parade of metal tureens, if we chose.

Grated cheese every day. I thought I'd gone to heaven.

The council estate was large, or certainly seemed so, and it was at times a frightening place for a shy and fearful child to live. But on the other hand, there was farmland and woodland accessible from the far end, and we would walk there with our dog Sophie, daily, often accompanied by an assortment of our cats. There was a particular meadow a barn owl quartered every evening and we'd go there in the school holidays to watch it. My brother found a monster one day on my mother's fuchsia bush, which we then discovered was an elephant hawkmoth caterpillar.

Every summer tiny frogs emerged from the pond in the back garden to make the journey into the overgrown lane behind the rows of houses, and I'd stay with them for hours, sprinkling them with water so that they didn't scorch as they crossed the burning tarmac.

When we moved to Wales we had big skies, no near neighbours, and over an acre of land. My parents rescued battery-farm chickens, and added a waddle of ducks and a blind gosling who grew up to be a very stroppy gander who thought I was his wife. We'd been poor when we lived in England but we were even poorer now, deprived both materially and socially as my parents shared hours at their unit in Cardigan market and relied on benefits to make ends meet. Only my father could drive, while the nearest large village with a bus stop was several miles away.

My natural timidity and introversion rose to the surface to become the dominant traits of my personality, and as my teenage years unfolded, depression, arachnophobia and anorexia got mixed into the soup. I spent a lot of my adolescence in my bedroom with my cat Sootica, reading or listening to the gentle, constant scratch and squeak of the bats who roosted under the tin roof of our cottage, inches from my head. Sometimes I'd tap and scratch a response, chirrup to them, and there'd be a short silence before they started up again. The sound comforted me through grim and unhappy evenings, instilling a life-long love of the creatures.

When people think *working class* they tend to think *urban*. They tend to think *industrial*. There's little mention of the rural poor. With the move to Wales we were suddenly without community, isolated and without the means or money to forge links beyond our patch of land. Outsiders. So I relied on the animals – the cats and dogs, the ducks and geese, and also the wild creatures that visited the garden – for distraction and companionship.

The nature books I came across in those years and in my young adulthood were educational and informative, written to instruct the interested, mainly by men. People who'd had the privilege of a good education, for others with similar educational privileges who could understand the scientific or Latin terms used. They were written for people with the money to buy those glossy books brand-new in the first place – for they were rarely to be found second-hand, and public libraries in rural areas aren't easy to access – and the money to visit the places mentioned. They were written for people with the money and means to buy the equipment needed to go out and study the natural world, and the spare time to indulge in it.

As a working-class writer and nature lover, one who was raised in rural settings with no access to money or to culture, I remember often feeling those books weren't written for people like me. They were erudite and enlightening, yet somehow detached. None of them gave me permission to simply *love* the wild creatures around me, to watch them and enjoy them; feel some kind of kinship with them. The emphasis was on understanding these animals and their private lives rather than caring about them: observing rather than sharing space. I puzzled over the ones I came across, leafing through my brother's *Life on Earth* by David Attenborough without much real interest and abandoning TH White's *The Goshawk* before I'd got halfway through. I was too young to appreciate the anguished state of the man, and I was horrified by the tortures he put the bird through. I felt the same horror and distress when I read Helen Macdonald's *H is for Hawk* decades later. I sympathised with her grief over her father's death but I couldn't get past the awful image of poor captive Mabel living her life out in Helen's living room. A beautiful, deadly bird of prey shackled and forced to live and fly by the whims and routines of her human owner.

Nature writing is still seen as a predominantly white, male, middle-class pursuit. Working-class naturalists are represented mainly in urban settings, finding jewels of life and wildness on their patch of housing estate or in the tight, green and brown spaces of a city. We are all encouraged these days to go out and hug a tree, bathe ourselves in the healing powers of the natural world. It's all about us. What the natural world can do for *us*. But for me, as ignorant as I still am about a lot of the animals I am besotted with, it's all about *them*. Meeting those wild lives on their terms. Not on mine. I don't fool myself that the bond I feel for them is reciprocated, and that's oddly liberating. I care so much, but for them I might as well not exist in any meaningful way. That frees me, maybe, from the ties that bind humans to one another, the sense of being beholden, of having to reciprocate. The love flows one way, without resentment or duty.

As I said, I'm not an expert. I simply love the natural world, the creatures who I happen across. I know that without them and the pure, deep joy that encountering them gives me, I would be deprived in ways more important than material ones; ways that are immeasurable and soul deep.

Beyond
THE GARDEN WALL

Mating Cuckoos by Foxhill Farm

We'd heard the cuckoo calling in a steady, patient tattoo of longing through the spring weeks before we saw it. He was somewhere on the outskirts of the village but not close enough to be able to pinpoint a location. After the initial excitement – in over a decade of living in St Dogmaels this was the first time that I'd heard a cuckoo – the sound soon became little more than a thread in the fabric of my days. I'd have noticed it, missed it, if the calling had stopped, but its very regularity relegated it quickly to the daily soundscape of my life.

We were deep into the first lockdown and both my partner Simon and I were working from home. Woven into the global anxiety of a lethal pandemic was the more immediate disquiet and difficulty of now having to share my every working day with someone who'd previously had an office to go to. And when the working day ended we had nothing else meaningful to do. Yes, we could (and did) drink more than was good for us and gorge on comfort foods whilst surfing the news channels – but we also walked. Thankfully the weather was kind and walking hadn't yet been made illegal.

At 5pm every afternoon we'd leave our desks, lace up our trainers and stride through the village to its boundary. We'd pass the LLANDUDOCH / ST DOGMAELS sign and head onto Cwm Degwel lane. This winds through a valley whose sides are steeply banked with slate; icicles string its peaks and rivulets in the winter months, and the midsummer sun only sears a narrow path of gold along it. We'd walk the damp and slender gorge, slightly uphill the whole way, until we reached a junction a couple of miles on. A right turn, and then another right, and we were suddenly on a wider, higher lane where the sky was all around us and the view unspooled for miles. St Dogmaels spread below us in a spill of rooftops and the Teifi estuary gleamed every shade of sapphire.

We used to walk this four-mile loop infrequently in the years before the lockdown, but now we walked it every day. Sometimes grimly – sweating and struggling on that gentle hill which swiped less than gently at our calf muscles after a day of work and worry – and sometimes with a deep and profound sense of wonder and pleasure. The thick drifts of wild garlic, which were low and tender spikes one week, would be ripe and pungent and overspilling the bank, the next. A grey wagtail might flirt its tail and surprise us as it swooped over the stream that ran alongside the lane, joined the next day by another. We noted the differences in the hedgerows and marvelled at how many changes nature could effect in a mere twenty-four hours, if a person really paused to take notice.

A pregnant vixen, one late afternoon, was curled asleep in a soft pile of undergrowth just beyond the wire fence that separated the lane from a tangle of woodland. The next, she was crossing the lane in front of us, shoulder blades scissoring sharply under her thin fur, and swollen belly stretched taut. She paused to nose at something in the bank and then heaved herself slowly through the hedge and was gone.

Sometimes we stopped at a gateway to say hello to a field full of horses, and every day I'd remember that I'd once again forgotten to bring a carrot to give them. Sometimes we'd sit on the warm tarmac of the dusty lane and just listen to a world that had lost the background throb of cars and planes. The tiny shifting life all around us that we could only now really appreciate.

Si, a committed carnivore, became fascinated by a herd of cows that gathered by the gate in one of the fields to watch us pass. He always stopped to stare at them, something like wonder on his face as they all gazed curiously at each other. He hasn't eaten beef since.

The cuckoo's call followed us around this meandering looped walk, and I felt for him as the weeks went by. His presence here was rare enough; to have the luck to attract a female seemed a wish too far. On my childhood council estate, several cuckoos would return to the area every spring and broadcast their availability to potential mates. It was the 1980s, and our estate rang with their call. I'd accepted the sound of the cuckoos with a child's sure and casual belief that they were simply part of the advent of spring, that they would always be there. It hadn't occurred to me to appreciate their presence as something that could ever be lost.

We were on the high, top lane when we saw the birds ahead of us, just outside the entrance to Foxhill Farm. It was another hot afternoon and we'd paused to capture that first glimpse of the hills and village tumbling down to the sea in the distance. At first I thought they'd been injured as they scuffled and rocked on the tarmac, wings colliding. And at first I thought they were a bird of prey that I'd never seen before. Some rare visitor blown in from the continent?

As we watched, they separated and one flew off over the fields. The other perched on the fence just ahead of us.

It hunched there, glaring at us from eyes the same fierce yellow as fire opals. We still didn't know what it was, whispering suggestions to each other – 'Surely it's not a kestrel? Could it be a hobby?' – whilst already knowing the guesses were wrong.

But then the cuckoo fanned his tail and leaned forward, and he began to call. Over and over, fixing us with his unblinking stare, he let us know exactly what he was. After a moment he flew into the hedge that divided two fields and continued his noisy staccato courtship of the female we'd scared off. Invisible now in the dense thicket of hawthorn and gorse, his voice followed us as we continued on our way.

When we got home I sat in the back garden and tuned in to the birdlife around me: the wren's furious, jubilant trilling; the collared doves wooing softly from the rooftop; the blackbird taking his position at the very top of the alder in preparation for his headline act: just as soon as the sun dipped below the horizon.

And beyond all this, somewhere a mile or two away, the cuckoo called and called. I hoped we hadn't scared his lady off for good or disturbed them before the deed was done. I hadn't realised how much I'd missed that sound, in all these years of not hearing it.

I hoped he'd return next year, and that I'd get to hear that sound again.

Juvenile Osprey on the Teifi Estuary

We sit on the lower deck of the Ferry Inn, our usual Saturday evening routine. Si, our friend Howard, and I. Dusk is beginning to smudge the air around us, an early moon raising itself lemony-sharp over the river. It's the second Saturday in September and despite the warmth, autumn is starting to dress the trees.

I watch the river idly as we chat. One of us makes the usual wistful comment about how wonderful it would be if we had an osprey here on the Teifi. I fret about Padarn – the last remaining chick on the nest at the Dyfi Osprey Project – worry about her father Idris who is several days past his usual migration date but bound by instinct and duty to stay with his daughter until she decides to leave. Howard reassures me that it will be fine, it will all work out. Another summer over. I'm secretly relieved to be at the end of it, to have followed a successful and uneventful osprey breeding season and be able now to release some of that incessant worrying that I can never quite reason myself past.

There is a flock of Canada geese gossiping on the far riverbank, hefty brown bodies shifting on brown mud, murky in the gathering twilight. As we sip our drinks and relax into the evening, one of the geese flies from behind the flock and up, landing on a low branch of the huge oak that guards the bend of the river. I start to raise an arm, point, and the goose, which isn't a goose after all, flies out across the river, hovers, dives, rises from the water and hovers again.

I stand up, still pointing. I can't speak.

Howard turns in his seat. 'Osprey,' he says.

She dives again, flailing on the surface of the water for a moment and then lifts clear and flies upstream. We can't see if she's caught anything. Si and Howard decide to stay on the decking and 'keep watch' (finish their pints) while I run home for my binoculars and then jog along the Graig – a narrow path that links one end of the village to the other – towards the Netpool green. Situated above the river with long views stretching up and downstream, I think it will give me the best chance of seeing her if she's perched somewhere along the bends.

And there she is, on a dead tree jutting from the steep cliff below the Graig. I'd passed her as I rushed along the path, only a couple of metres above her and unaware. I watch through the binoculars as her head ticks up and down swiftly, rhythmically, her top-of-the-cream chest capturing the last of the light each time she straightens. She's caught something. It's small, but at least she's caught something.

I phone Howard and tell him that she's here, that she's eating, and then I walk back along the Graig to The Ferry. It's nearly full dark now, a strain to focus through the binoculars, and I'm happy to leave her to her fish supper, happy just to know the Teifi has provided her with a meal.

As I take my seat on the pub decking, she appears around the curve of the river, flying low, and lands in a dead tree on the far bank. We order another round of drinks and stay with her as she preens, taking turns to peer through the binoculars even after the night has folded fully around us and there is no longer anything to see. I think she'll probably be gone in the morning, taking on the next stage of her migration, and I want to squeeze every moment from this evening.

There is quite a crowd at the moorings in the village the next day. Howard had posted news of the osprey on a local wildlife Facebook page and a throng of photographers and bird enthusiasts have arrived. Scopes and camera lenses are trained on the same dead tree across the river where she must have roosted overnight and is still perched now.

She's unringed, so probably a Scottish bird, as the majority of known accessible nests in England and Wales ring each year's chicks. And she's in full juvenile plumage, cream trimming her feathers: a youngster on her first migration, most likely female, judging by her size. She can't be much over a hundred days old.

People stand shoulder to shoulder and stoop for a look through the telescope that has been set up for communal use by one kindly soul. We chat with strangers and send messages to friends and neighbours to come down. The atmosphere is vibrant, generous, and Howard would have made a killing selling tea and coffee from his house – he lives right on the moorings – if he'd thought to set up an impromptu café.

It's a drizzly Sunday, cooler than it has been for weeks. People mill around all through the day, anoraks zipped tight and cameras the length of a rifle hoisted over shoulders. I charge from one end of the village to the other, back and forth, following the river up and downstream as the osprey flies towards Poppit beach, returns to her dead tree for a while, and then heads towards Cardigan town where she isn't seen for the rest of the afternoon.

We end up back on the lower decking of The Ferry in the early evening: Si, Howard, and I. The sky has lowered to meet the river, the world now greyed and shapeless, thick with oozing rain clouds. We are the only ones out there, huddled under an awning. We raise a glass to the osprey, to the magic of the last twenty-four hours, and wonder whether she's now moved on after a brief stopover to rest.

Si goes inside to the bar to get another round, and Howard and I sit in the gloom and twitch our binoculars up to our eyes every time a gull flies past. A moment later he leaps up and jabs a finger past my face. 'There she is.'

She drifts along the riverbank, pale and wispy as a ghost in the twilight. She's level with the top deck of the pub, a few feet from us, as she hovers and then dives fruitlessly for a meal. It is too dark and the river too muddied from rain for her to divine if there are any fish for catching.

She rises from the water, shakes herself vigorously, and floats above our heads. If we'd been on the upper deck we'd have been able to reach out and touch the tips of her wing feathers as she passed us. There is a second as she flies over our heads, barely stirring those huge wings, when she sees me, looks through me, and flies on. She disappears around the bend of the river, and she doesn't circle back and return.

Si emerges from the pub, jostling glasses between his palms, and we leap on him and tell him what we've seen, how close she'd been.

That was her last hurrah, we decide. She's definitely gone now. What else is there to stick around for, when the urge to migrate is like splinters in the bone?

I stay at my desk working the next day, relying on Howard, with his enviable view, to let me know if he's sighted her. *Nothing*, he reports back at regular intervals. *She must have gone.* My relief is profound. I tend to over-empathise with wild animals, over-bond with them, and as little as it helps me, it helps them even less. The previous year a violent early-summer storm had rolled over the Welsh osprey nests, forcing the male birds to find shelter on low ground and the female birds to hook their talons into the nest and grimly hang on through the gale-force winds, totally unmoving for a day and more as they strove to protect their precious tiny chicks from harm. Unable to leave the livestream and abandon my vigil, I'd watched with a panicked, overwhelming impulse to bear witness to their struggle. It had felt like the least I could do.

When the winds dropped and Aran – the male osprey at the Glaslyn Osprey Project – returned to the nest it was clear he was injured, unable to fish. Over the next two days their three chicks died, one after another. On the Dyfi nest, the youngest chick died. I'd watched – along with hundreds of other viewers from the safe comfort of our homes – in horror and despair, becoming increasingly obsessed and desperate until I'd finally forced myself to switch my computer off and back away. The anxiety that I work hard to contain daily was out of its box and spurting like a firework, my every waking thought focused on those nests and their dead chicks. I was embarrassed, too, by how easily my equilibrium could be undone by events that were totally beyond my control, queasily suspicious that there was something humanly arrogant or narcissistic about my distress. With or without my attention, those wild lives either continued or they perished. My tears wouldn't save them.

I decide to take a walk after work, to check for myself whether this juvenile osprey has really departed. The rain has stopped and the sun is back: another glorious afternoon. Pausing frequently to scan any likely-looking trees I wander along the Graig to the green, passing the occasional forlorn photographer who's travelled a distance to the village just to see her.

Until you are lucky enough to witness an osprey in flight, and experience just how big they are, every large pale-morph buzzard, every passing black-backed gull, even the odd heron, could be mistaken for it, certainly at first. And an osprey can be mistaken for those other birds, at a glance. But I have a lucky knack for homing in on the tiniest anomaly in a wider landscape, separating it out from its background and revealing a shrew or a tree creeper or a deer. Or an osprey. I'm convinced I'll find her if she's still here, and if I don't, then that will mean she's gone.

The trees that line the far shore along the curve of the green are still shaggy with leaves, bronzed here and there with delicate touches of autumn makeup. I lean against the wooden fence and scan them, my focus relaxed and soft. One of the branches shifts slightly, turns its head, and I narrow my eyes, raise my binoculars, then phone Howard to tell him that she hasn't gone after all, she is dozing in a patch of sunshine right here in the centre of the village. He rounds up the photographers who are waiting at the moorings and sends them to me.

Explaining her precise location to other people proves hard work. *You see that clump of lighter foliage on the tree directly opposite us. No, the other one. Okay, go left a bit and up. Follow where my finger's pointing. Hang on a second, she's turned around again so you can't see her white breast. See where that magpie is. Just go down a bit and right.*

There is one dead tree off the netpool green that could have been made for an osprey's fishing perch. Its branches jut at different angles and heights over the water, shiny and pale as whale ribs rubbed clean by the sea. It is to this tree that the osprey flies, nap over and audience gathered. She lands for a moment and watches the river with a fierce intensity, then flies out and hovers, plunges. The slap of her body hitting the water echoes around the slate banks. Cameras click up and down the green, and people gasp and murmur.

She hauls herself up and out, hunched on the bank for a moment, then flies back to the tree and repeats the process. Soaked through now and suddenly gaunt and fragile, bones like a bundle of twigs beneath her flattened feathers, she shakes herself in midair and returns to the tree. Flies out, hovers, and plunges into the waves that are still rippling out from her last dive. By this point any fish she might have caught would have long since scattered to safer waters. Though I'm watching her with besotted attention, a sharper interest stirs: *she isn't trying to catch a fish; she's practising the skills needed to catch fish.*

Juveniles depart for their first migration without having ever fished for themselves – the learning curve on their journey to west Africa is steep and harsh, often fatal. This girl, with her intense concentration on the physical acts of hovering and diving, has begun her migration but paused it here in order to learn and hone her fishing skills. Despite the less-than-ideal village setting, and the respectful but substantial audience she's gathered, she is going to keep practising until the actions settle into her muscles as memory and start yielding proper meals. Enough fish to build her up and fuel her onwards.

We all watch until exhaustion ends this day's fishing lesson, and she flies upriver, never having once glanced our way or shown any interest or concern in us. It is as though we exist on a different plane from her, hidden behind a veil of humanity.

The days settle into a routine: I stay at my desk, working while Howard sends regular updates from our favourite bench that is tucked into a corner of the moorings green.

> *She's dozing on her tree.*
> *She's just flown to Poppit.*
> *She's just come back.*
> *She's headed up to Cardigan.*
> *Fish!*

As soon as I've finished work I'm back at the moorings with Howard, feeling a sharp tug of need: to see her, to be close and watch over her. We haven't yet seen her actually catch a fish, but if she flies low over the river and dips her talons in the water, that means she's eaten and is cleaning the fish scales off and I go home happy to know she's fed. If she's mobbed by corvids or gulls, chased away from a fishing spot, I'll be left despondent, the near-constant worry for her crashing through me.

September gives way to October, the days shortening but still as warm and sunny as late summer. We meet every Saturday evening at the Ferry Inn to toast another week's anniversary: one week, two weeks, three weeks, four. More often than not on those celebratory evenings, our osprey will fly past to roost in her dead tree on the far bank, and sometimes she pauses at the river's edge for a vigorous bath, the sunset catching the water as it cascades over her, turning her into a rainbow. Every day I look up when I'm in my garden pegging out washing or feeding the birds, and often I'll see her flying over, trailing a fret of gulls.

One Sunday morning as the sun burns through the mist that drifts over the river, she lifts herself from her usual dead tree opposite the moorings and sky-dances, flying up vertically and then flipping over onto her back, tumbling towards Earth and then looping back up. It seems to me, with my human eyes, as though she is simply having fun, enjoying the warmth of the sun, a full stomach, the power of her wings.

I take a week off work in early October and spend my days with Howard at the moorings, dashing home to bolt lunch or feed the cats, dashing back out again and then staying out until dusk. I have a novel to edit and a looming deadline for a short-story commission, both priorities for my free time, but my attention is entirely on the osprey, my concentration lost to anything else. Si, when he returns home from work, doesn't need to phone me to ask where I am; he just appears and joins us on our bench.

During those hours, as we wait for her to appear or watch her dozing in a tree, the Teifi offers up its other jewels. We see a kingfisher every day, fishing from the end of the jetty, and curlews wade past, flute tucked under a mottled wing. Howard helps me improve my woeful ignorance of estuary birds and I begin to really notice them for the first time. 'Little Grebe?' I ask, when a tiny bird pops up on the surface of the water like a cork released from a bottle of fizz. A quick glance, a nod and a smile. 'Redshank?' as a bird on burnt-orange legs picks its delicate way over the mud.

One morning, looking skywards, I see what I assume is a thrush flying overhead, mobbed by crows. It weaves and pirouettes through the air, evading its persecutors effortlessly. I point up at the scene, realising then that this thrush-sized bird could only be a merlin, for why else would the corvids dislike it so much? We watch as the drama moves swiftly away, high over the fields behind us, and disappears into woodland.

I've been friends with Howard for a few years, recognising from the moment we met a kindred spirit with a mutual love for wild creatures. We meet regularly at the pub to chat – he and Si often the ones doing the talking, discussing cricket or music while I watch the river flow past – but it's only now, during these intense weeks of companionship, that I feel I really *know* him. The easy shared silences, the exchanged confidences, the eye-rollingly bad jokes. I don't have to explain myself, hide the extent of my love for the osprey behind a more socially standard, more detached interest. With him I can worry incessantly about her without being seen as obsessive or strange, and his calm reassurances are a comfort that grounds me through the passing weeks.

On the last day of my holiday, late in the afternoon, our Teifi girl appears from the direction of Poppit and makes her way slowly upstream; hovering, dropping a few feet and then catching herself before the dive, flying on a little way and then hovering again. The tide is low, the river strung in thin, stretched channels between the sandbanks. When she reaches the moorings she hangs in the air while she scans the water, huge wings working to keep her still.

She plunges and hits the river with a splash. Her wings are spread on the surface of the water, beating hard to lift her clear. She rises a foot or so, something huge hanging from her talons, and then drops back down and is submerged. She tries again, flailing on the surface as she struggles to get airborne.

The panic lasts less than a minute but feels so much longer to me standing on the shore and watching her. Though it's rare, ospreys have been known to drown when fishing, and this fish is clearly proving more of a meal than an inexperienced osprey had bargained for. I spin on the balls of my feet, ready to run to the jetty and from there jump into the river and wade out, but she manages to lift clear of the water and fly in dips and jerks – the weight of the thrashing mullet dragging her down – over to the far bank.

My legs are nerveless now and I have to sit on the bench for a moment. I think of all the other fish she must have caught these last weeks, all the future fish she will catch if she survives this first year, the potential for danger and the prospect of death with every attempt.

The corvids flow out from the trees lining the far shore and surround the osprey, an endlessly shifting cloak with one objective. They tag-team, working to distract her, to irritate her into lashing out; dancing towards the dying fish in quick, sharp pecks and then rising in a raucous cloud of torn mourning weeds, resettling. We watch through binoculars as she spins and lunges, giving more of her attention to the crows than to the fish, unable to focus on the meal she's worked so hard for. On the still air a faint quacking reaches us, a series of high, stressed chips, and then that quacking noise again. I recognise the sound from my years of watching the different osprey livestreams: a corvid-specific alarm call.

I message Si, and a couple of friends who have yet to see her, and we all stand and take turns looking through the binoculars. When she finally decides to ignore the harassment and concentrate on her meal, the corvids settle patiently around the osprey, muttering occasionally to each other, diving close to peck up a scrap of flesh or innards but otherwise abandoning the decision to torment her. There will be supper enough for everyone if they wait long enough.

She is still eating when we leave her, two hours later. It's too dark now to see much of anything other than the steady tick of her head going up and down as she feeds, and she's showing no signs of declaring herself full and abandoning her feast. As we say our goodbyes and go home, I think the corvids will probably have a lot less in the way of leftovers than they'd predicted.

I'm in the shower a couple of weeks later, rushing through washing my hair so that I can make the most of this sunny Saturday morning and join Howard at the moorings, when my mobile rings and then rings again. It beeps with a message. Beeps again with another. *I bet that's Howard saying there's two ospreys now*, I think idly as I dress quickly and pull my phone from my dressing gown pocket. *Now wouldn't that be a drama.*

TWO ospreys!!! the first message says.

TWO OSPREYS!!!! TWO!!!! the second says.

I sweep up my binoculars and a mug of coffee, shout to Si, and tear from the house with my soaked hair streaming behind me.

Howard tells me the story as we sip coffee and cling to our binoculars, raising them to our eyes and saying 'Gull,' to each other every time a large bird with sharply hinged wings appears around the bend of the river. He'd been sitting on the bench watching our girl as she preened in her usual dead tree opposite, when an osprey had drifted up from Poppit, hovered for a few minutes to look for fish, then drifted back downstream towards the beach. Seemingly unbothered, our girl had continued with her ablutions and then flown off. For a moment, Howard hadn't registered the presence of the stranger, had simply thought *there she is* before the inevitable double-take.

We message friends while we wait for either or both of them to return. It doesn't take long. First one and then another osprey appear from the direction of the beach, both circling lazily above the river, passing close to each other without displaying any apparent signs of aggression or concern. I compare sizes: roughly equivalent, so probably both female? The unringed newcomer is also dressed in full juvenile plumage, her breast a vast shock of pure white; easy to identify when compared to the neater, more muted creamy breast of our original Teifi girl. There is something surreal about standing in my home village on a sunny mid-October Saturday, watching two members of my favourite bird of prey. After all, these creatures were persecuted to extinction in England and Wales centuries earlier, and, despite conservation efforts, are still a recovering species, not yet stable. And yet here they are, pursuing their lives without any awareness of the joy they are giving to the people who watch them.

Finished with the business of looking for fish now, our girl returns to her dead tree and begins to emit the short, crisp intruder chips that are osprey specific. Intruder alarm calls I've only ever heard before on the livestreams and in the vicinity of a nest. I've always wondered whether they make those calls away from their nest, away from their territory. And now I know. Surely that means our girl sees this stretch of the Teifi as hers, which will bode well for a return to us if she survives the migration.

As the newcomer seems to be unfazed by the intruder chipping, our own Teifi juvenile leaves her tree and flies over the river, circling the other bird in tight figures-of-eight, escorting her away from the area. They fly upstream and out of sight in polite convoy, and then a few minutes later our girl returns and spends a good half an hour bathing in the river in front of us before returning to her tree to keep watch.

The newcomer is back the next morning, and the entirety of that day is spent watching one or both of them flying around the moorings, perching in trees, attempting to fish. Late in the afternoon as I head home, I pause in the lane and turn back to look.

There on the far bank, two ospreys perch in separate trees close to each other, both facing out so that I can see their breasts: one cream, one white.

The last couple of weeks before she finally leaves to continue her migration, the Teifi osprey makes some significant changes to her daily routines. She spends much more of her time deep in the gorge near Cilgerran, where the river loops in tight, narrow bends, merely flying over the moorings on her way to the beach or pausing briefly in her usual tree for a preen before heading off. On sunny days she'll circle over the village, catching the thermals and rising higher and higher until she is no more than a speck of dirt on a camera lens. I think she's finally preparing to continue her migration, and though I'll miss her – I missed her already since her decision to spend less time on this stretch of the river – I know I will be euphoric with relief when she's left. An osprey couldn't survive a British winter: daylight hours are too short and the fish go too deep so the bird would starve to death, and she should really have gone some weeks previously. There have been a couple of perfect windows over the last fortnight, the wind blowing hard in the right direction, but she hadn't left when the leaving was good and I'm starting to worry that she won't leave at all.

There had also been an unsettling encounter with a juvenile goshawk, which had spooked her out of the magnificent dead tree on the Netpool green one day when she tried to fish. Though a part of me had been thrilled – a goshawk here in the centre of the village, a bird I'd previously only associated with deep woodland! – it's cause for worry. Goshawks are apex predators and will kill an osprey; the knowledge of this overlapping territory between the two birds is disquieting.

A few days before she leaves, she returns to her old moorings haunt and catches a huge flatfish. The afternoon is drizzly and cool, finally jacket weather. I watch with Howard as she hovers and dives into a river muddied and swollen by recent rainfall. There is another moment of queasy panic as she struggles to raise herself clear of the water, my palm pressed hard against my mouth and my knees liquid, but she manages the ascent and flies upriver to the bend directly beneath the huge oak – to the very spot I'd first seen her, seven weeks ago.

We rush with a photographer friend to the top of the Graig where we'll have a relatively close and clear view of her. The photographs he takes of her eating on a tree stump, surrounded by rabbits and a squirrel, the inevitable corvids, have a fairytale quality to them. One in particular I return to regularly, to glut myself on the exquisite mosaic of her underwings, angled sharply up and out, spread wide to balance her as she wrangles with the fish. The delicate patterning and the colours, squares and swirls of toffee, creamy marshmallow, chestnut: it's one of the most beautiful images I've ever seen.

The friend shows me photographs he'd taken of her when she first arrived and then flicks through to the photographs he's taken just now. 'Look at the size of her,' he says, 'compared to how thin she was back then.' I stare at them, click back and forth, and feel a ludicrous, teary pride. She's achieved so much since she arrived here, acquired so many vital skills and given herself every chance of surviving into adulthood. She's ready to go.

The weather has finally tipped towards autumn, the nights longer and chillier, and gathering storms queuing up in the Atlantic. A couple of days after her flatfish feast, I see my osprey for the last time, briefly and from a distance as she flies briskly past on her way to Poppit. I don't see her return, though I wait for another glimpse. Is this to be it? Such a cavalier goodbye, and such a stark lack of acknowledgment for my weeks of adoration. My mood is melancholic, gently wistful, as days go by and there are no sightings other than a fleeting one over the Marshes on the thirty-first of October. She's finally left, then.

As I write this it's been two months since those magical seven weeks. I still look skywards with longing when I walk the lanes from my home to the moorings, before catching myself in the remembering: she's not here. My heart still lurches for a second when I see a bird perched in her favourite tree. Until I remember that she's gone.

If she survived her migration then she'll return as a two- or three-year-old. If she survived, then she'll surely come here, to this stretch of the Teifi, to the river and the landscape that imprinted itself on her during those seven stopover weeks when she learned to fish and look after herself, become an adult bird.

Skydancing Ravens at Cwm Gwaun

It was a cool, sunny March morning. We – Si, his cousin Sparky, and I – drove up and over the moor that skirted the Preseli hills, negotiating alarming hairpin bends on single-track lanes that were no wider than our car. We paused in a passing place high above the sea from where we could see our destination far below us. A dark ribbon of woodland down on our left. Cwm Gwaun.

We took in the near view, admiring the austere, timeless landscape of heather and scrubby grass tuffets that stretched for miles in every direction, the jutting rocky outcrops as small as a footstool and as large as a bus, speckled yellow and silvery green with lichen. A sparrowhawk sped past the car at knee height, swerving fast onto the moorland just ahead. It flushed a skylark up from the ground and pursued it, streaking between the rocks and out of sight. Around us, other birds rose and scattered in a frantic burst of alarm calls. I couldn't avoid the inevitable pang of sorrow and sympathy for the skylark and its precious, precarious life, wearing the melancholy essentially and lightly as we pulled back out onto the lane and continued on our way, plunging down into the valley.

Si's cousin Sparky is a wonderful finder of new walks for us all. A keen birdwatcher, he prefers the coastal settings of shoreline and estuary and can sit and watch the wading birds for rapt hours, so this four-mile loop through ancient woodland was a treat more for me than him. But if he'd rather have been elsewhere, he didn't let that show, and I always looked forward to his good-humoured companionship on walks.

I'm rarely happier than when I'm surrounded by trees, and the Gwaun valley itself is a strange, otherworldly place. A narrow, steep cleft carved into the landscape by retreating glaciers in the last ice age, Cwm Gwaun rises above the walker in an unchanging, unspoilt bark tapestry; its heavily wooded banks fold around you in a way that's oddly comforting. There's an aura of magic here that I've never experienced anywhere else; a kindly magic, with none of the forbidding, bleak atmosphere of the Preseli hills or Carn Ingli.

We got out of the car in the tiny car park at the bottom of a steep hill, and Si and Sparky began the process of sorting out boots and rucksacks while I walked out from under the deep shadow of the huge overhanging oaks – still bare and bony, not yet blurred at their tips with new growth – and looked around me. It was late morning and the sky was a pale, faded blue. A long way above me, about a dozen ravens – my favourite corvid – flew and tumbled above the ridge.

As I watched them, one bird would shift a little and reveal – beside it or beneath it, or above it – another bird. So around two dozen ravens, then, twice as many as I'd initially thought. Their sound reached me as I focused fully on them; that wonderful harsh, hollow croak. They flew in pairs, surging vertically upwards and then spinning down, wingtip to wingtip or covering each other's bodies so that they merged briefly into one larger bird before separating.

I called Si and Sparky over and we all stood and watched as the ravens danced with their mates, affirming or reaffirming their bonds before the hard task of breeding and raising chicks began. They spilled over the sky, rasping love songs to each other, spiralling and looping together as instinctively and easily as if they could read the other's mind. And I'm sure they could.

The walk through the wood was lovely: carpets of wild garlic no more than tight young spears promising a rich release of scent in a few weeks; early primroses studding the banks. And all the time that faint *cronk* followed us as the ravens called out to their beloveds.

They were still dancing when we returned to the car a couple of hours later, loving each other before the chicks arrived, while they had the time and energy to spare.

Nightjar at Cross Inn Forest

In hindsight, choosing the longest day of the year to try and see a bird that is nocturnal wasn't the most sensible decision I've ever made. We set out on midsummer night at around 7.30pm, collecting Sparky en route. It was a beautiful evening, the light blued and soft as sea glass. The world had that timeless everlasting-summer feel to it, where you can't imagine it ever raining again, can't imagine a day where you could be cold under grey, damp skies.

There is something about the nightjar that has always captured my romantic imagination. Perhaps because I was a depressed teenage goth, drawn to all creatures of darkness. Or perhaps because, as with the bittern, I long to *hear* them as much – if not more – than I long to see them.

In my cloth bag, along with a couple of bars of chocolate and a flask of water, I'd folded a tea towel, on Howard's advice. 'If you wave a sheet or something around above your head,' he'd told me, 'then they think it's another bird and swoop down over you to get a closer look.'

I'd never been to Cross Inn Forest despite once living not far away, first in Aberarth and then Llanrhystud, for a few years when I worked for Social Services in Aberaeron. My free time back then was spent wrangling the two large rescue dogs I had, and walking with boisterous dogs doesn't generally entice wildlife to show itself.

When we got out of the car – the sun still riding the sky and twilight a long way off – every midge in a five-mile radius headed over to say hello. *Every* midge. Fighting through clouds of them, choking on the first of many who seemed strangely drawn to the inside of my mouth, I pulled my hoodie on and cursed the lack of insect repellant. I hadn't even thought to bring any along with me, which was seriously remiss, given my fraught history with biting insects and their exuberant lust for me and my blood. Even Si and Sparky weren't getting off lightly, both starting to slap and scratch at their arms.

Despite this horror, our collective mood was cheerful, fizzing with anticipation. We struck out along the main path, passing a couple of small groups of people who were also doing the midge dance with their arms. One of the groups stopped to chat: they too had gone there for the nightjars but were now on their way home after an hour spent walking around fruitlessly. Two of the women, wrapped in beautiful silky shawls, held glasses of wine which they sipped from as we talked. Now *that* is good solid preparation, I thought, admiringly. They might have turned up a few hours too early to spot a nocturnal bird, but they thought to pack wine.

As we still had another hour or so until dusk, we decided to wander without direction or intent, just aimlessly meander along the paths through the patches of clear-fell and deeper forest, past the little streams and pools of standing water, pausing when we felt like it. Absorbing the smell and sight and sound of the place.

Juvenile redstarts provided us with an escort, twitching along the tree line from branch to branch and then landing on the track ahead of us, taking off again almost immediately and returning to the safety of the trees. Sparky insisted on stopping at every sighting, raising his binoculars – 'It's another redstart, Sparks. Honest,' and then lowering them with a nod. 'Redstart,' he'd say.

I tried to slow myself down, making a conscious effort to adopt some of Sparky's leisurely, ambling spirit. I've always walked fast, my stride naturally long, and I have an anxious need to *keep going* until I reach my destination, a guilty aversion to relaxing in case I'm seen as lazy. I had to remind myself that here, tonight, we were merely killing time until it got dark enough for the nightjars to show themselves. If we decided to stop for a snack or paused at every single sighting of a bird that I could tell at a glance was a robin or a blackbird, then so be it. Nobody would be judging me.

There was a heath to our right which we circled around, and a cuckoo called somewhere, over and over, from its wild tangle of scrub and stunted trees. The air was fragrant, almost sticky, as the cooling heather released its herby scent. We reached the T-junction where the nightjars had been seen and heard the previous week, struck out to the right and wandered along that path; returned and took the left branch. It was gone 10pm now, and the evening was starting to gather around us, the sunset an artist's palette of peach and rose smeared across the sky.

10.30pm, and we'd been walking for two hours. I hadn't truly realised just how light a summer's evening is when you're not watching it from your lit home or garden. Outside, and without the background glow of streetlamps or houses, it felt as though darkness was always just beyond reach. There'd be a slight dimming of the light every twenty minutes or so but it was still essentially more day than night. Si and Sparky had fallen behind, chatting happily and noisily, and I'd reverted to my default behaviour, marching on ahead, alone. I wanted some distance between us all, worried that I wouldn't hear the nightjar if it started churring; I didn't know how loud it would be and didn't want to miss it.

I cupped my hands behind my ears and walked like that for a while, stopping to spin in a slow circle, straining to hear anything unusual. A cuckoo kept up his steady calling and an owl started its plaintive, fractured hooting somewhere close by. The midges redoubled their efforts to consume me.

At 11pm, Si said that we'd need to start thinking about going home. It was a work night for all of us and we had a thirty-mile drive ahead. I changed my tactic then, dragging behind them both, slowing us all down. Whenever they realised I'd fallen back, they'd stop and wave me along, reassuring me that we'd come again next week, or soon anyway, and look one more time. I stooped to re-tie laces that weren't loose, paused and held my hand up with exaggerated drama – 'What was that?' – and all the time willed a nightjar to appear *right now*. I felt an urgency that was vast and irrational.

When we got back to the small car park it was gone 11.30 and a muted half-moon was heaving itself into the sky. I cast looks back into the forest. If I bolted now they wouldn't leave without me, would they?

An older couple loomed out of the gritty dusk as we were unlacing our boots beside the car. 'You looking for nightjars?' the man asked. 'There's one high up in that tree there.' He pointed to a large tree by the side of the lane. 'We come here most nights to see them.'

It was now, finally, too dark to make anything out, but we stopped packing our things into the car and stared up at the tree, straining to see *anything* among its thick and leafy branches. I stepped away from the others and stood alone in my own pocket of darkness, vibrant with renewed hope and silently pleading with the bird to show itself.

When it started churring, the sound was so loud, so unlike anything I'd ever heard before. It was organic, but not birdlike. Eerie and *other*. I imagined if someone encountered it, walking alone in the dark and not knowing what a nightjar was, they'd have felt a thrill of sudden, ancient fear in the same way you would if something howled deep in the woods in a country which has no wolves.

'Carly, can you hear it?' Si whispered to me. I'd moved further away from the group, back into the forest, and he couldn't really see me, didn't want me to miss this. I stood with my face tipped up to the sky and just listened as the churring went on and on. No recording could come close to capturing the experience.

The sound stopped with an abrupt suddenness. One moment the noise was everywhere, and then it was nowhere. I stayed frozen, straining through the now-thick night to try and see the bird. 'There you are,' one of the older couple said, triumphantly. 'Told you it was there. Off he goes, look.'

The nightjar swooped from its tree and towards me, glided over my head and away into the pitch depths of the forest. It seemed to float on the air with only the merest shiver of its wings, its flight as unbirdlike as its song. As if it were a gauze and silk puppet in a child's play, suspended on invisible strings that fluttered it weightlessly over the stage above the enthralled audience.

Bittern at the Teifi Marshes

I'd seen from posts on social media that a bittern had been sighted at the Teifi Marshes, the nature reserve a mile away from my home. The bittern is a rare visitor at any time, and even more unusual for having arrived in the middle of summer.

I've always wanted to see one. And, more than seeing it, I've always wanted to hear a bittern boom. The best wildlife encounters are the ones you don't plan for, the ones that fate and lucky timing throw in your direction, but this was too good an opportunity to miss.

The main path through the reserve runs parallel with the Teifi river through the wetland section and on to the wildlife centre. Dotted along its length with pools, hides, and creeks, this path bisects the reed beds. The bittern, a reed-bed dweller, would have any number of places to hide and none of them accessible to humans, but I figured that if it could be sighted then it would be found wherever the crowd of photographers was gathered. We just needed to head for that.

And we saw them from a way off: a sizeable group of people gathered at the fence in the centre's car park right at the heart of the reserve; some intense folk with cameras and some curious casual walkers.

'Bittern?' I asked one of the photographers.

He glanced at me and nodded – half acknowledgement as we were both local and vaguely recognised each other, and half answer to my question. 'It's down behind the pond there.' He pointed. 'You won't be able to see it without a lens.'

Si had his binoculars and we took turns squinting through them. Even with the magnification we could only make out the outline of the bittern's head as it stood frozen a distance away, neck stretched and rigid, body submerged in the reeds. It apparently hadn't moved for some time. A squatter, browner, shyer relative to the heron, it was endearingly emu-like in its belief that standing very, very still and staring up at the sky protected it from being spotted by predators.

The less dedicated watchers wandered away after a while, leaving space for the people left behind to fan out a little. I sidled into a gap and leaned my elbows on the wooden gate, scanning the marshy field idly for the water buffalo who spend their summers on the reserve and are often to be found queuing inquisitively around the fence line, their velvet-mitten ears flapping away flies. Si offered me the use of his binoculars again but I shook my head. Until the bittern moved there was really nothing to see, and when it moved, the photographers' reactions would tell me where to look.

I have binoculars and they're invaluable for spotting the creature you know is there but can't quite get a fix on with mere human sight, but if at all possible I don't ever want there to be a filter between me and the wild world I'm watching. Even if that means a less clear, less sharp focus. Even if that means no record of an experience other than the memory you carry home. I really can't imagine having anything better than the memory. Nature, for me, is there to be smelt and seen and heard, and above all loved. Not framed, zoomed in on and then dismissed.

A thick clump of undergrowth directly in front of the gate, and just to my right, started to shake. I prodded Si and nodded downwards. We watched as the undergrowth quivered and the tiny, pointed tip of a conker-brown nose nudged into sight then disappeared. Without even needing to glance around, I could judge by the tense stillness surrounding me that the bittern was still non-compliant and the sum focus of attention, so I leaned down a little, the better to view the creature that was watching the humans.

A head popped up quickly, bright black eyes scanning the line of people. It ducked below view. Popped up again, eyes now fixed on me. 'Weasel,' I whispered. 'Weasel.' The best wildlife encounters really are the ones you don't plan for. The ones that fate and lucky timing throw up.

I looked around, eager to share the excitement. A row of blank mechanical eyes faced me, a bank of high-lens cameras with only one goal. 'Weasel,' I said, as an impossibly long body – crisp white bib trailed by russet cheeks and spine – shimmied out of the clump of grasses and paused for a second, balanced on a trembling thistle, before scuttling across the earth in front of us and disappearing into the hedge. The black tip of its tail hung in the air for a second before being whipped away and out of sight. Si and I were the only two people not buried behind a lens: the only two people who'd seen it.

Cameras began to whirr and click around us and the group of photographers surged forward as one. The bittern was finally on the move. It rose from the reeds and flew across the pond, away into the deeper safety of the reserve. As I watched it flail ponderously through the air, I marvelled at the heft of its body, the ungainly shape of its air-borne form. In flight, it was so much bulkier than I'd expected it to be.

One day, I hope I'll be able to catch a bittern's boom. Until then, it was enough of a treat to have seen this shy bird, albeit briefly. And Lady Luck threw in the weasel for free.

In the
GARDEN

Runty

My brother joined me at the back door as I stood and watched the birds at the feeder. The jackdaws were starting to flock into the garden, landing on branches of the hawthorn and shaking loose drifts of blossom. If I didn't keep running out there, clapping my hands and scaring them away, they'd strip the feeders in under an hour. They'd remove the lid from the fat ball feeder to dig out its contents, swing from the peanut holder until it gave under their weight and scattered nuts all over the patio. I usually let them have a few minutes to plunder what they could before I began the tedious and frustrating task of chasing them away, over and over and over, so that the smaller birds might have a chance to feed.

'Do you reckon that one's Runty?' my brother asked, nodding towards a jackdaw that was fixing us with its icy blue and impudent gaze while it waited for its turn at the sunflower hearts. We stood and watched for a moment as it lost interest in us and jostled for a better position. There wasn't even a flicker of recognition. No slight nod of gratitude. I hoped that one was Runty.

'We did a good thing there,' Kelvin said. 'With Runty. We saved his life.'

A few years earlier a family of jackdaws had fledged from my neighbour's chimney pot. The youngsters' raucous clamouring for food had kept me enthralled through May, whenever I was in my back garden; the occasional tantalising glimpse of a surge of bobbing heads leading me to think there were at least four chicks squeezed into the narrow pot. Similar scenes were playing out along the terrace as other chimneys were utilised by other jackdaw families, and I was thankful for the warm weather which meant none of my neighbours were inclined to light fires in the evening.

When the fledglings emerged from their cosy home, spilling out onto my neighbour's roof to yell at their parents and practise flying, I could see that one of them was far smaller than its siblings. Patches of its gaunt body were featherless, scabbed and sore looking. It clambered around the rooftop, begging for food from its parents, who largely ignored it and devoted their attention to the larger, healthier birds. Its siblings pecked at it with a cruel and visceral repulsion, a rejection of its obvious weakness which they couldn't allow to become *their* weakness. There's nothing altruistic about jackdaws when survival is a tightrope strung thin as cheese wire. The focus has to be on maintaining your own balance.

Every morning, before I'd even turned from the feeders to start back down the path to the house, the newly fledged jackdaws would be all around me, eyeing me from the hawthorn and taking swooping, clumsy dives at the feeder to be first at the goodies. Little Runty – as she became known – watched from the rooftop, chattering to herself, calling piteously for food that didn't arrive.

And then after a couple of days she took the plunge and flew to the feeder with the rest of her family (and all of the other neighbourhood jackdaws). But she didn't pause a short distance away to eye me warily and coldly, waiting impatiently for me to leave. She crash-landed on my feet and waddled over them, resting against my ankles and gazing up eagerly.

I stooped and said hello, and carefully spooned a slurry of oats, soaked sultanas and mealworms onto the ground beside her. I watched over her while she ate her fill, then I spooned out another mound. One of her waiting siblings scolded me loudly, seemingly incredulous at this misplaced sense of priorities, and I told it to have patience. That act of flying to me, which was in all reality merely a case of bad coordination and a lack of skill on Runty's part, had released a fierce protective instinct. For as long as she'd let me, I would make it my mission to feed this scabbed, frail bird and keep her as safe as I could without compromising her wildness.

Intervening in this kind of situation is anathema for wildlife purists, and I do understand the reasoning. There may well have been a deep and insurmountable flaw in Runty's genes that would mean she would sicken and die in her first winter anyway. Maybe there was something wrong with her cognitively which would mean she would never be able to look after herself. What would I do then? My elderly tabby cat would be no threat if they had to share domestic space, but was I prepared to care on a long-term basis for a wild creature with disabilities whose specific needs I knew very little about?

I was working as a freelance editor at the time and had just finished a large commission; I had the luxury of a few weeks off before the next deadline. I called out to Kelvin, who was staying with us while he looked to rent a house locally, and gestured down at Runty – Kelvin insisted she was a he and should be called Kojak because of the bald head, but as neither of us knew the sex and I'm the one writing this, the name I gave stands – stumbling and scrambling over my feet, cheerfully exploring the laces of my trainers as a potential food item. Kelvin had been following the narrative of the young jackdaw family along with me, sharing my distress at the pitiful sight of Runty when she fledged, and the merciless way she was treated by her kin.

'Could you bring out a tin of cat food?' I asked.

I forked out a decent amount of my old tabby cat Hobbit's gourmet, very expensive 'slow-cooked beef stew' cat meat onto the ground, and we both watched, grinning at each other, as Runty gobbled the lot down. Full now, probably fuller than she'd ever been in her short life, she winked her pale eyes a few times until they closed fully, and then she shuffled down onto her stomach and settled into a doze. I stepped gently away from her but stayed close by, fearful that she would be attacked by the other jackdaws or by another corvid if I went indoors.

We devised a plan between us, Kelvin and I: while the weather was warm and dry and we both had time on our hands we would devote our days to feeding Runty and keeping her safe. We couldn't do anything about the nights – I was insistent that we didn't try and tame her and bring her indoors unless we absolutely had to – but we could at least give her all the help possible during daylight hours. And the bird herself had enough awareness now, enough of an instinct for survival, to stay a safe distance away from the clatter of jackdaws who hadn't ever shown her acceptance.

Over the next few weeks, while I'd still be shuffling blindly around and nursing my first coffee, Kelvin would come indoors to let me know that Runty had eaten her entire body weight in cat food and meal worms and was now sleeping it all off under the garden chair. When I went out mid-morning to do my usual feed for all of the birds, she'd awaken with a jerk and scoot over to me, flying with a floppy, hoppy gait beside me along the path to the end of the garden.

After I'd filled the feeders and scattered food on the slate slabs for the ground-feeding birds, I'd gently nudge Runty from my shoes and ladle out her brunch. I'd stay with her, or Kelvin would, until she'd eaten her fill, and then she'd be escorted to the shade of the monstrous hydrangea to rest. One of us was always close by, or the kitchen door was open; should there be a screech of distress or a whirl of feathers in the garden, we were there within seconds, bumping into each other as we burst up the path.

In the long, light evenings, she returned to the neighbour's roof where she'd leap around in the tawny sunset and burble to herself, try to tag onto the edges of her siblings' games. When dusk fell, she inserted herself back into the safe, familiar chimney pot for the night.

Within a week I noticed that the other jackdaws had stopped bullying her. They're clever birds and they saw that she'd been elevated in the flock, given special status by the humans who were doling out the daily meals. For whatever reason, she was no longer a liability. If she got a platter of gourmet treats three times a day then maybe they would too, if they showed her suitable respect.

Within two weeks Runty's feathers began to prick through her healing flesh and lay themselves over her frame in sleek, thick folds. She started to spend time with the wider flock of birds, separating off at mealtimes to get her special plate of food but otherwise flapping clumsily around after her family. In the evenings she was no longer a lonely figure hopping about by herself on the neighbouring rooftop: other jackdaws spent time with her, eyeing me greedily as I watered the garden, waiting for the late-supper snack that would surely arrive.

After a month – early July now – it was hard to tell Runty apart from the other jackdaws. There were still a few patches of grey skin visible on one side of her neck, but she was almost unrecognisable from the thin, bald bird she'd been at the point of fledging. Her eyes no longer bulged like a gothic creature from a Poe story, monstrously large in a face pecked raw and bald, the skull surprisingly small without its covering of feathers; she no longer stumbled over her own feet when she moved around the garden or flew from the rooftop.

In the mornings, if I was tardy with organising breakfast, she'd fly to our bedroom skylight and peck at the glass, scraping and sliding down the pane before scrabbling back up to the top of the frame and peering in. Sometimes the other jackdaws would join her, the dawn peace rudely shattered by a gang of rowdy teenagers, swearing and jostling as they trampled a noisy path through our dreams.

At the end of that summer it was impossible to tell Runty apart from her kin. She was glossy, full-feathered. She no longer came to me for food, preferring to maintain the detached distance the other jackdaws showed, waiting for my back to turn and then diving onto the feeders. Though I felt a pang of nostalgia at times, a wistful and sentimental desire for the vulnerable young bird that had needed me, I was proud of what Kelvin and I had done, proud that we put her needs first and never attempted to tame the wildness from her. It would have been so easy to pick her up that first morning, hand feed her, bring her inside.

And now, when I stand at the back door and watch the jackdaws flock into the garden, I have no idea if she's one of the clatter. She'd be an old bird now, if she hasn't already died. I looked it up and jackdaws live until they're about five, so she's in all likelihood dead. Maybe one of her offspring is brooding the clutch of noisy chicks that are currently in my neighbour's chimney pot. As I'll never know, I'm going to pretend that's the case.

Steak Dinner for Four

While I was looking for something in the freezer I found a large T-bone steak, half buried in compacted ice and bags of vegetables. It had been in the bottom compartment for several months now, since the previous Christmas when Si had bought it (for an eye-watering amount of money) from a farmer friend.

I asked him whether he was finally going to cook it and eat it, or whether I could give it to the badgers.

'I don't want to eat beef anymore,' he told me. 'Let the badgers have it.'

I hauled it out and chipped the ice away, set it on a plate in the kitchen to defrost. I've been a vegetarian since I was seven, and the sight of the blood pooling beneath the huge slab of flesh as it began to soften made me squeamish. I poked a finger into it after a few hours to test its readiness, took a knife to it a couple of hours later and sawed four large hunks from the thick bone that bisected it. Now to wait for dusk, and the feast.

I've been feeding badgers in my small garden for about a decade now, since they started making it a stop-off point on their nightly foraging route. Their vast, ancient sett is in a privately owned field behind our house, surrounded by woodland and protected by landowners who are dedicated animal lovers.

I'd discovered all my spring bulbs had been dug up and eaten

Tapdancing Tawny Owls

Our bedroom is up in the loft, tucked under the pitch of the roof with a large skylight puncturing either side of the slate tiles, front and back. One view gives us a slew of houses with the Teifi estuary snaking behind them and the other view – which might actually be my favourite – gives a panoramic sweep of the field and woodland behind the terrace. In the spring, when the trees are still skinny and naked, I can lean out and call my cat for his breakfast and watch him tense and turn to home, flatten and lengthen himself in the long grass and then run like the wind from the very top of the field. His three legs working like furious pistons, not missing a step. Throwing himself towards his next meal.

The skylights are open most of the year, and in the summer months I can hear the badgers below me in the garden, snuffling and snorting their way through their snacks. In the winter months, the screaming foxes in the field jolt me and my heart from rest to a panicked, confused fear from which I rise and must switch on the light and roam the house, count heads of cats before I realise that the sound of something being murdered is actually just the sound of something wanting to mate *right now.*

I lie there most nights through the dark hours with a cat sprawled across my thighs or my aching bladder, another cat curled, snoring lightly, in the armchair in the corner of the room. Sleep, for me, is not an easy thing to capture. But I'm very good at lying very still and pretending that I'm asleep. If I can kid myself for long enough then maybe my busy, anxious brain will be lulled into relaxation and loosen its grip, let me go for a few hours.

Until Crow, who is the one usually sprawled across my stomach, decides to have a vigorous wash, elbows working their torture on my organs.

A week before midsummer, some point past midnight. Crushed and fretful beneath the swollen, damp weight of the humid day that clings to the air in the bedroom despite the open skylights, a sound jolts me from near sleep to alarmed consciousness. A loud bump from the loft hatch above me, followed swiftly by another. There is a scuttling and a scraping back and forth. *Rats*, I think despairingly. Rats must have somehow got into the tiny few inches of space between the bedroom ceiling and the roof. Maybe one of Crow's less desirable gifts has made a bid for freedom and managed to find a way up there. How am I going to evict them? I don't mind them living at the bottom of the garden but there is no way I'm prepared to let them move into the house.

As I lie there, stiff with anxiety, the noisy, somewhat clumsy, pattering and scrambling continues above my head. And then the night is ripped apart by a screech so urgent and so close it could be in the room, right beside me. Before the sound has faded, and while my heart is still trying to crawl out from the back of my throat, there is another shriek. And then another. A high-pitched, throbbing scream, fracturing at the edges as if the breath were being choked from some frantic creature.

I know then what the sound is: a hoot-off between two young tawny owls.

They stay on the roof for the next hour, inches from the top of the open skylight, practising their hooting. Every time one or other of them lets out their unearthly, splintered yell it speeds my heartrate back up to the danger zone, my breathing threatening to quicken to the point of overwhelm. But despite

the panic attack – and I'm getting better at greeting the fl
physical sensations with acceptance, folding them into my
as opposed to fighting them – I smile every time one of th
starts out strong but then finishes its effort with a hoars
croak, its sibling taking the lead with a flourish of cracked y

The session ends when a distant hoot from the par
properly executed and grown-up hoot from the field behi
terrace, summons the youngsters. Does the adult have a
them? The next lesson on their journey to adulthood is w
They scrabble and clamour their way off the roof and fly a\

They return every night for a week and I get used to the
and the manic scrambling above me when they land on the
I steel myself to accept and enjoy the onslaught of callin
will keep me awake and in a state of hyper, frantic alert th
the dark hours. I think of them out there, only a couple of n
above me and probably still juvenile enough to look like ad
leaking feather pillows, trying so hard to be adult raptors, beli
that the louder they shout the more grown up they are.

one morning; the birds' water bowls tipped over; wiry twists of mottled grey and black fur snagged like iron wool on the edge of the slate step that leads to the back of the garden: a perfect scratching spot. A few nights later I heard something snorting and snuffling around the bird feeders.

I scattered a few peanuts around the feeders one dusk. The following night, I added a stale heel of bread and some leftover boiled potatoes. I started sitting out on the sun terrace above the kitchen in the evenings to watch for them and was soon rewarded by the sight of a striped face nosing its shy way into the garden from under the fence. Another black-tipped snout close behind.

Our garden, like most of the gardens in St Dogmaels, is set into the hill and tiered. There are steps from the kitchen door leading up into the garden, and another set of old stone steps – now without a purpose, for humans at least – set into the bank at the far end, leading up to the land beyond. The terrace where I live was originally built for the staff of the old village workhouse which stands on a huge plot about half a mile away, and the steps were a shortcut for these staff, leaving by the back door and crossing the field rather than having to go out the front door and around the lanes. It's these mossed, slippery old steps that the badgers use every night to reach their snacks, flowing down them like tubby slinkies.

I've been asked by people in the past why I don't try and 'make friends' with these badgers. Tame them, essentially. For wouldn't that be a wonderful thing, a real party piece: a pet badger. It is such a depressingly human trait to see the wild and want to know it, master it, make it *less wild*, which would then signal some obscure victory for the tamer. A world made safer and more understandable, maybe. I remember seeing a documentary or a news segment when I was a child: an older man (to my child's eyes a very old man) sitting in his living room while badgers came and went through the open door. Some settled down by his feet for a good scratch while others nosed around for food or bickered with their family group. He'd lean down to stroke one of them, scold another fondly.

I could imagine the sense of awe and privilege, the wonder, the man would have felt when these persecuted, secretive creatures began to trust him and rely on him. And there would have been a degree of puffed-up pride as well, an ego well stroked. I can see how a person could start down that road of taming wild animals, *for their own good, to keep them safe*, but even at the age of eight or nine, my primary feeling was horror rather than delight or envy. I needed someone to tell me what would happen to the badgers when the old man died; who would look after them then? Had he appointed a younger guardian who would devote their own life and home to the welfare of these animals as wholeheartedly as he had? For they now had human handprints all over them, they were no longer the wild things they once were, and probably would never be able to make their way back to that natural, uncontaminated state again.

The handprint I've left on 'my' badgers is so light that they don't even know I'm there most of the time, and if they get a hint of my presence then they turn tail and run from me. Though I'd have a much better view if I were to sit at the very front of the sun terrace, or even down in the heart of the garden itself, among the flower beds, I keep my distance and I don't speak to them. Just sharing the twilight with them is enough: glimpsing their hefty waddle around the garden; listening to the chomp and snort and grunt as they eat and the soft whickering noises they make to each other; the sometimes blood-chilling squabbles over a prize piece of apple.

When they find something they particularly like – Bonios or an egg are real favourites – the badgers will always storm off with it to eat in private. On my camera trap I've captured images of six adults at a time browsing the slate slabs peacefully together, and I've been lucky enough to see three youngsters feed alongside two adults a few years ago: the (I assume) parents standing by and tolerantly allowing the excited, boisterous cubs to squeak and snuffle and growl over carrot sticks and peanuts.

Occasionally, if I'm late with my plate of food or if they're earlier than expected, the smell of them will be all over the back of the garden where the bird feeders stand. Intensely, sweetly, musky and musty, the smell catches in the back of my throat like a solid thing and brings saliva flooding into my mouth. It's so *animal*, so unsanitised.

Maybe the best thing I could do for the badgers is not to give them these snacks at all but let them wander my garden and focus on the plant bulbs and fallen seed instead. Let them forage more naturally and work for their food. The same argument could be made for the birds whom I feed daily and take such pleasure in watching. I'm aware that there's something hypocritical at play in my reasoning why *my* engagement with wild creatures is acceptable, when surely any engagement is essentially about nothing more than selfish human gratification.

I comfort my guilty conscience with the thought that if I were to die, or move away, the badgers wouldn't miss me and they wouldn't suffer my loss. The snacks are just that; being deprived of them wouldn't mean the difference between surviving or perishing.

I laid the four big chunks of meat down on the slate slabs and retired to the sun terrace. It was a beautiful autumn evening, the sky purpling as the sun dived down behind the shoulder of land that always separates our village from truly spectacular sunsets. A sharp, skinny moon showed itself over the Teifi. I'd bundled up in a coat and laid a blanket over my knees. A glass of wine rested on the table beside me. It could be a long wait.

The magpies came first with their portable typewriters tucked under a wing, hitting the same key over and over in the hawthorn tree then swooping low over the meat, gathering their long capes and swirling away when I stood up and waved my arms. I could hear distant whickering and squabbling; the badgers were out of the sett and making their leisurely way down through the field.

The pair of crows who'd raised two chicks nearby – adorable things with their fluffy-punk heads and death stares – came next. They were less inclined to be chased off and I had to resort to clapping my hands and standing at the edge of the sun terrace until they gave up waiting for me to go inside, and swept away.

Something large shifted in the gorse and bramble thicket beyond the garden. I tiptoed back to my chair and settled down, took a sip of wine.

It was getting chillier now, shadows creeping out from behind the plant pots and laying themselves down around my ankles. I'm never prepared for autumn evenings, the abrupt way from mid-September onwards the light is squeezed out of the sky, after the slow honeyed trickle of the summer evenings. Winter, though still a way off, now feels like a near reality.

The shifting sound became louder, the heaving and squeezing

of heavy bodies through the brambles and under the fence. A striped face appeared briefly, narrow snout lifted to the sky to sniff the air and divine whether it was safe to advance further. There was a moment when I thought the badger had sensed me and was going to retreat; it stood frozen, turning its head slowly from side to side, half-submerged in the tall grass on the high bank atop the stone steps. But he – it was the huge boar badger – decided it was safe, or maybe he could smell the beef, and he emerged fully, sliding down the steps and out of sight behind the shaggy rose arch, into the belly of the garden.

There was a startled snort and then he reappeared, stampeding up the steps with a hunk of steak in his mouth. He hit the gap in the fence at a run and I could hear him thrusting through the undergrowth to a private spot where he'd be able to eat in peace.

Before the noise of his retreat had started to fade, another striped face appeared at the top of the bank. No pause to check the coast was clear for this badger, it must have seen or smelt what its mate had made off with. It slithered down the steps and snuffled out of sight for a moment, then scrambled back into view with not one but two pieces of steak in its mouth, head held stiff and high to keep the meat off the ground. It stumbled and dropped one chunk, tried to retrieve it, but as it loosened its jaws, it dropped the other. Growling at the world, it grabbed for the nearest piece and fled in a panic.

The boar badger had hurried back to claim another piece of the steak. He met the other badger at the very top of the steps, the two bodies cannoning into each other with a dense thump. There was a brief, noisy tussle and an awkward shoving back and forth as each tried to push past the other on the narrow ridge of the bank, then the badger with the steak vaulted over the steakless badger and ran. The boar badger sprinted down the steps, reversed backwards when he realised he'd just rushed past a nice chunk of meat, snatched it up and retreated.

There was one piece of steak left. I was sure the large male would be the one who claimed it. In the years they've all visited my garden this boar badger, this giant patriarch, has always been there. To my human (and therefore half blind) eyes he's never appeared to age, to slow down or become less dominant in the group. Always first in to select the prime food items, bossing the others without seeming to bully them, he is a true beast.

I met him up close one summer night, rushing along the path to the back of the garden just after dusk with my plate of peanuts and apples. I was late and he was early, and I tripped over him as I leapt over the step and onto the slate slabs. I don't know which of us was the most scared but I suspect it was me. Backing away from each other, me painfully conscious of my fragile, bare ankles – remembering my father's stories about how badgers will lock their jaws when they bite prey or fight, and don't unlock them until their teeth meet – I cooed soothingly as if he were a fluffy little rabbit and he snorted to let me know he was wild and frightened and therefore unpredictable. Once there was the entire length of the (really rather small) patio between us, he took his eyes off me long enough to deduce that he could escape before I reached him, and he ran. I scattered his dinner around me and retreated smartly to the house, before he could return and change the narrative.

It was the boar badger who took the last piece of beef, as I predicted. With his previous two fillets of steak either lodged in his gullet or stashed away somewhere secret and safe, he stormed back into the garden and tumbled down the steps. Ignoring the peanuts and carrots, and a lovely selection of local windfall apples donated from neighbours, he seized the meat and then ambled back up the steps with it. There was no need to rush now. He was home and dry.

The steak dinner for four had fed two (but mainly one).

When I told the story to friends afterwards I added a dramatic flourish: that night would surely go down in badger folklore as the best feast night of their lives. The Night of the Steak Dinner. They'd be passing the tale down through the generations to their great-grandchildren.

And maybe one day, little ones, if you live long enough and you're very good, that night will happen again.

Des Res

If I'd realised before the female had laid her eggs, then I'd have blocked the hole up and put an end to their inadvisable scheme before it started, but it took a few days of being peripherally aware of the wren shouting from the rose arch before I fully absorbed what he was up to. By then it was too late; he was in and out of the jagged little hole in the wall by the back door every hour or so with wisps of feather, a dried parcel of moss. I thought maybe, hopefully, he was making a nest more as an invitation for a female, rather than having a mate already in residence. But either way, I couldn't block the hole, just in case.

Two days later a faint cheeping could be heard from inside the cavity, and the wren was suddenly always there; back and forth every minute or so with a beak crammed with insects. The couple had flown so far beneath my usually sensitive radar that they'd managed to incubate the eggs to hatching without me even being aware. Evenings stood at the sink washing up, I'd been no more than a couple of feet from the female, brooding her precious clutch just the other side of the wall, with silent patience. And now I had a nest of chicks beneath the tin roof of the lean-to by my kitchen door, tucked under the flight of steps leading up to the sun terrace. Easily accessible – from multiple angles – to any passing cat, rat or corvid.

My four cats, alerted immediately to the sound of the chicks, prowled beneath the nest and watched with disapproval as my brother Kelvin and I lined the back of the open stair-treads with plastic mesh. It wasn't a professional job but I thought it would work to stop them wriggling through and onto the roof of the lean-to, where a determined paw would then be able to reach the nest. The mesh gaped at the sides so the adult wren could still fly through easily, though when it was time for the chicks to fledge, I thought it could pose a problem. But that was a problem for another day; right now, my only task was making the nest impenetrable.

The lean-to roof posed more of a challenge. The cats couldn't jump up onto it from the ground, but they could easily access it from the tiered garden. I collected large plant pots, pieces of slate and chunks of quartz rock I'd pilfered from various coastal locations years previously – before I'd realised it was illegal to remove them – and piled them onto the roof. I added every tray we had in the kitchen, an old kettle, a folding chair, a pair of Si's walking boots that he'd left out in the rain and I thought he probably wouldn't wear again, two watering cans, and a small table. Studying the access points from below, by the door, and then above, from the garden and sun terrace, I thought it might just be enough.

And for the next few days it did seem to be. The cats would gather outside the back door after their meals to gaze yearningly at the hole six feet above their heads, or they'd occasionally attempt to negotiate the thick obstacle course on the tin roof – often getting wedged halfway through the thicket of assorted barriers and having to reverse back out with a high-stepping, embarrassed lack of grace – but they soon gave up when I shooed them away and waved the water pistol threateningly in their direction. I felt a sense of tentative triumph. This was stressful but manageable. One day at a time.

I'd written in my diary when I thought the chicks had most likely hatched, and I looked up when they were due to fledge. The window seemed unduly vague: *between fourteen and nineteen days*. When one goes, they'll all go, the smallest alongside the largest. There was differing opinion on how they'd go, whether it would be a case of flinging themselves from the nest and flying away immediately with their parents, or a more gradual process of hopping around until they found their wings. I suspected the latter, having a hazy idea that, as wrens are largely ground feeders, they'd be similar to blackbirds once fledged, and not take to the air immediately or with any great skill.

The adult seemed either immensely trusting of us or simply immensely practical, having thrown his lot in with mine. He'd fly into the rose arch every minute or so with food and scan the garden for danger, then spy one of the cats – often curled up a distance away and minding their own business – and start yelling. The sound brought me to my feet and away from my desk immediately. I'd go outside and assess the situation, carry away any cat that was too close, and wait for the wren to break cover. He'd quieten down as soon as I appeared, and fly to the nest, thrust his head inside to feed the young and then perch at the entrance for a moment, eyeing me and singing a few notes, before flying off. By the time I'd returned to my desk he was back on the rose arch with another meal, shouting the odds, and up I'd get again.

I've always loved the wrens' song above any other birds. That vast, sweet sound emerging from the throat of such a tiny creature. But though I often heard them, I'd never had such close views before, only occasionally seeing one briefly in the garden scuttling through the undergrowth, busy and mouse-like. Now I had the privilege of sharing direct space with one, studying the delicate layering of minute fawn and toffee feathers over a frame so small I'd probably not be able to register the weight of it in the cup of my palm if I held it. Where I'd previously thought they were simply *brown*, almost drab, I could see now the many shades of brown and marvel at the intricate mottling of cream and hazel across wings that in sunlight appeared almost azure.

We hadn't seen the female at all, folded as she was around her fragile chicks in the darkness of the nest. I wondered how many there were; what the nest itself looked like. The photos on the websites I looked at showed beautifully woven things, deep and oval. Like a woollen hat dropped and then slashed at the crown to create an entrance. I imagined my cats' fur providing some of the inner lining, a soft smatter of orange and black keeping them all snug.

Every day the sound of cheeping strengthened and grew more strident. Even when I was indoors, I could hear it and knew from the sudden rise in ardent chirruping when the chicks were being fed. The weather was miserable, wet and chilly, and the cats stayed inside for day after day, allowing the male wren to go about his essential business unimpeded. That didn't stop him from announcing himself with his rattling alarm call, a maraca shaken violently, every forty seconds or so, sharing with the world just how cross he was with everything. The force of his alarm-calling shook his entire body and travelled through him to the foliage he was perched on, jerking a branch of honeysuckle up and down, back and forth, so that it was still vibrating after he'd left it. Once he'd made his displeasure fully known he flew in, fed his family, and then departed to forage for another meal.

And we continued like this for a few days, with the sound of the chicks and the sound of the male's drilled fury ringing in my ears, ricocheting around my head, until there was no sound left but theirs.

The female wren emerged from the depths of the nest once her chicks were about a week old and could be left alone for periods of time. They were impossible to tell apart, these adults – identical in looks and equally bad tempered – but now we had twice the volume at mealtimes. Which was every forty seconds. The weather had improved and after work I sat outside, spending the late-afternoon hours scooping up cats and depositing them elsewhere, then standing guard by the back wall and telling the wrens to *hurry up and stop wasting time shouting, just bloody feed your offspring while the coast is clear.*

There were four beaks visible at the entrance to the nest now, surging forward and gaping wide, shrieking their need whenever a parent hove into view. The faces belonging to these huge yellow beaks were not much bigger than my fingernail, prickly with growing feathers, still more dinosaur than bird. I couldn't imagine how they'd be ready to fledge in just another week or so, it seemed an impossible leap from this vulnerable dependency to that. In the late evenings both parents would take a rest together on a bare branch of the hawthorn that jutted out above the shed, perched side by side and exchanging their views. I felt an embarrassed need to apologise for the din they made – scolding any bird that dared to fly into the garden, scolding each other, then flying off to one of the nearby gardens and scolding whichever neighbour had the temerity to go outside – and a defensive desire to explain the situation to everyone I saw on the street.

After dusk there was a silence so complete I could barely trust it. The usual night-time hubbub from the garden and the field beyond – squabbling, chomping badgers and calling owls – was still there but so much less immediate, so muted compared to the hours of urgent sound I'd endured all day, and so it faded to nothing. Si and I would sit in the living room and watch something for the hour before bed and I'd raise my hand every couple of minutes for him to pause the programme. I'd strain towards the alarm calls I could have sworn I heard, but then shake my head. 'No, sorry, it was in my ears.'

At bedtime I'd go outside and stand in the darkness for a few minutes, leaning against the wall beside the nest, making sure none of the cats had decided to take on the challenge of the obstacle course on the lean-to roof while my back was turned. Mere inches away from me, four tiny wren chicks stirred and shifted inside their home, letting out a sleepy cheep now and again.

The people I told about my unconventional house guests tended to divide themselves into two camps: those who advised me without much interest to 'let nature take its course', and those who shared my sense of joy and anxiety. The former camp was bemused that I would go to such lengths to safeguard the nest or waste so much of my day worrying about the birds, and the latter camp could be relied on to step in and take on the task of 'wren duty' without quibble or raised eyebrows when we had to go out for a while and leave the family unprotected.

Those last few days before they fledged were fraught with tension and a dizzy exhaustion. The collective noise the family made had now reached epic proportions and the chicks spent hours taking it in turn to hang from the nest entrance, watching the narrow strip of world that was their future or fixing me with a beady, unblinking gaze. It seemed they'd gained their feathers almost overnight; they were proper little wrens now. I bought a hanging plant basket and secured it from a nail below the nest so that if their exuberant rush to be first to a meal tipped them out then they would have a safety net of sorts to break their fall.

At around 5am every morning I'd be woken by one or both of the adults bawling from the rose arch. I'd be up and downstairs before my eyes had fully opened, chasing away a magpie that had taken to hanging around on the fence and showing a worrying interest in the nest, and then I'd stay awake to stand guard with my first few coffees of the day until it was time to start work.

I tried not to think too much about the logistics of the fledge itself, but now that it was close a knot of dread had settled in my stomach. What if they decided to go at dawn when I was asleep? Or when I was in a meeting, or in the shower? In the seconds it would take me to run outside there could be full-scale slaughter. Seconds would be all it took. And to add an extra layer of stress, Si and I were getting married in a few days' time. Kelvin was on stand-by to come over and stay with the wrens should they still be in residence while we went to the registry office, and I'd written lists, told him the best way to help them fledge: folding back the plastic mesh and removing some of the upended plant pots that lined the steps, to give them a clearer flight path towards the garden. But, mildly hysterical from lack of sleep and looming panic, I was starting to doubt that they would ever leave. This was my life now.

The rains returned and the temperature dropped again. I checked the weather forecast hourly and noted the potential dry periods, preparing myself for the possibility of a fledge. One night, after the adult wrens had gone off to roost and the garden was silent once more, I stood outside and listened to a strange, rhythmic whirring and rustling coming from the nest cavity. I worried that a rat had got into the wall but there were no sounds of distress, and a quick sweep with the torch showed no sign of external damage. An hour later and it was still going on. Then I realised what it must be: the chicks were exercising their wings, furiously beating them in the cramped space, in readiness for the jump from the nest and the start of the rest of their lives. The next dry day, I was sure, would be the day they fledged.

After I'd signed out of work the next afternoon I went to lie down. Though it was the middle of July, it felt more like October. The rain had been heavy for hours, the wind spitefully cold and gusting high enough to sway the garden fence. Barely 5pm, and yet the sky was scratchy with an early dusk. I tried to nap but the wrens suddenly started shouting and didn't stop. I knew the cats were all indoors, for why would they venture out into this? I called out to Si to check what was going on and after a moment he called back to me to come and have a look for myself.

Huddled on the kitchen step, already soaked through, was a vibrating, cheeping ball of feathers and bright yellow beaks. Five beaks, five wren chicks, who had decided to plunge from their cosy nest into the worst possible weather. Five, when I'd only ever seen four. The smallest was half the size of the largest, blindly following its siblings as they scattered behind the pots of lobelia and sweet peas in search of their parents and then scattered back out and past me, into the lean-to. Back out to hop behind the pots again.

The next five hours were a blur of standing at the kitchen door and watching them in despair, or running around in the rain, desperately scooping them up and putting them back in the nest only to have them ping immediately back out. The adults flew in every minute or so and fed them by my feet but made no attempt to lead them away. All of the stories I'd read online about how quickly and easily the fledge would happen – one moment they're there and the next they're gone – were fairy tales of the kind you read to children. This was a fairy tale of the original kind: grim, bloody and cruel. That tiny fifth chick, far too fragile to be braving the world, broke my heart over and over as I watched it struggle to reach its parents, tripping and stumbling and always last, always missing out on the insects that were shovelled into other eager beaks.

The cats, who were hours past teatime and panicking at being locked inside, took turns to howl and throw themselves against the door to the kitchen where I was imprisoned, as I couldn't open it and risk them stampeding through to the cat flap and freedom. Their distress fed mine and I put my boots back on and went outside again, determined to try one more time to get the chicks away from the house. I managed to pick up three and carry them up the steps to the back garden, and the remaining two followed in a series of fluttery leaps. Then up the path and the last two steps onto the slate patio right at the back of the garden, beneath the hawthorn. I lifted the tiniest chick onto the shed roof and left it there, calling piteously for its parents, and it was soon joined by the two largest, who were starting to realise what their wings were for.

I watched as one of the adults flew into the hawthorn and began to sing, calling its young up into the branches of the tree. It was getting too dark, the rain too heavy, to see how many followed, but when I checked half an hour later they were all gone, and after that only one adult returned to the garden with food for the two remaining chicks. These two were huddled under the honeysuckle, trying repeatedly to climb it and reach their parent who called and sang from the top of the fence. But they were waterlogged and cold, weakened by the efforts of the last few hours, and every time they tried to get up into the thick canopy of the honeysuckle they fell back down. I went outside again to try to pick them up and help them on their way but they scuttled under shrubs and disappeared.

Si eventually managed to lift one of them up and insert it into the thick, fragrant crown of the shrub, just beneath its waiting parent. The other disappeared under the hellebore. It was full dark now, there was nothing more we could do. I was soaked through, in a state of high distress. Nothing had prepared me for the reality of a fledge into those weather conditions, for the sight of those tiny, water-logged creatures so utterly determined to survive. We told each other we'd done everything possible, far more than anyone else would have done, and it was finally over. We could leave the house again. We had our lives back and we could go and get married without worrying about what was happening here in our absence.

The next morning was warm and sunny. One of the adults appeared on the fence above the honeysuckle with a beak full of insects. The last chick clearly hadn't yet left the garden. I kept the cats in and waited, staying indoors myself so that I wouldn't disturb the pair. And after an hour of frequent visits the wren stopped singing and disappeared. The garden was silent. The last chick had gone. It really was over.

Pumpkin Eyes

The young vixen appeared late one spring. She unfolded herself from the flower bed and sat slouched on her haunches, yawning and eyeing me as I wandered up the garden path with the birds' food. I stopped and stared. 'Hello,' I said. 'You've flattened my aquilegias. They're not coming back from that.'

She inserted a paw into the thick fur behind her ear and had a good scratch, then stood and stepped delicately over the squashed flowers to join me on the path. Together we filled the bird feeders and scattered seed and peanuts around. I cleaned the bird bowls and filled them with water. Refilled them again after the fox had had a good drink.

I left her out there, nipping peanuts from the slabs with dainty precision, and watched from the window for a while. She returned to her flower bed and swivelled in tight circles like an ice skater, gliding over the earth, before curling up and tucking her pointy nose into the velvet pocket behind her jutting thigh bone. I was bemused but delighted, unsure whether to chase her away so that she understood that humans are not friendly creatures; we are not to be trusted.

I knew foxes visited the garden at night alongside the badgers, but daylight sightings had always been brief: a flicker of auburn in the corner of my eye as they fled at the sight of me. Only once had I seen cubs in the field behind our house, spying a tumble of squat red bodies a couple of years earlier, led by their thin mother into the shadow of the dense undergrowth. She'd trotted in a fast, straight line across the grass, intent on reaching safety, while the cubs had leapt and pounced in her wake. Every thistle needed to be sniffed, every tail of the cub in front needed to be chewed and worried at.

Hobbit, my beloved feline companion of sixteen years, had died three weeks earlier and I was grieving, lonely without him and without animal companionship. There was a yearning part of me – a superstitious, romantic part – that saw this beautiful fox's arrival in my garden, her calm and familiar treatment of me, as *a sign*. Of what, I had no idea, but foxes are tricksters after all: guardians of the liminal space between our world and the underworld.

Foxes really suffer the prejudice of humans. Viewed as sly and vicious, untrustworthy, they're persecuted – from what I've observed – even more than badgers. Shooting them, or trapping them in cruel ways and allowing them to suffer agonies of terror and pain before they die, is commonplace. Their frenzied and panicked slaughter of every single chicken if they manage to get into a coop is seen as evidence that they're murderous, bloodthirsty creatures, without qualm or conscience. Killing *just because they like it*, as I've been told. The reality is that they're simply overwhelmed by the sheer wealth of food in front of them and their instinct is to kill it all *now*, while it's there. To shore them up against the lean times.

Demonised for being wild creatures, for merely following their natural wild impulses, it's no wonder rural foxes are shy around humans, reluctant to show themselves in daylight hours.

Which made the appearance of this young vixen even more puzzling and even more wonderful. I watched her through the day as she sprawled comfortably among the flowers, rousing occasionally to have a wash or look around lazily before settling back down. When I went outside, she flowed up onto her paws and watched me intently, head on one side. She followed me as I weeded the garden, stopping when I did, sniffing at the plants I piled beside her. She settled down by my feet when I sat out there with a book which I couldn't read because I was too busy staring at her.

She left in the evening, slinking through the fence into the field behind the garden while I was cooking dinner, and I thought that would be the last I saw of her.

She was balanced on the steps of the back wall the next morning when I went out to feed the birds, rump cocked in the air, head low over her front paws. She'd appeared as soon as she heard me, and she huffed a greeting and wiggled her tail before threading a way down the mossy steps to my side and sitting beside me, expectant for peanuts. I gave her the ones I'd been planning to tip into the feeder and went inside to get some more. I added a big lump of cheese. I thought she'd probably like cheese, because who didn't?

And that day was spent the same way as the previous one, with her lolling in the flower beds and then following me around whenever I went outside. I texted Simon to pick up some sausages when he was in the supermarket after work. I thought she'd probably like sausages too.

I was doing what I'd vowed never to do: I was engaging directly with this wild creature, planning treats that would keep her close. I was fascinated by her.

I'd never before had the privilege to really study a fox, to absorb the sight and smell of one. I watched her intently as she reclined by my side through those days and weeks she spent with me, marvelling at all the tiny details that made her so perfectly fox.

Small and delicate overall, her tail was almost as long as her body and her fur was the colour of apricot jam. Her paws were tiny and near black. Her muzzle was long and sensitive, slightly pert, framed by a dark ruff of whiskers and tipped by a shiny black paint-splash nose. Her eyes were the exact shade of pumpkins. When she turned those eyes on me, gazing at me searchingly, I cursed my human lacks, my inability to divine what it was she was trying to tell me. For she really seemed to be trying to communicate something.

Her smell wasn't as sweet as the badgers', and not as pleasant. It caught the back of the throat in the same way, but there was a sour taste left on the tongue when she gave herself a good scratch and the scent was released in thick drifts that hung on the air. Her habit of squatting to pee or poo wherever the mood took her was less pleasant too. But the upside: the rats who'd been

establishing a fiefdom in the back of my garden since my elderly cat got too frail to terrorise them some months earlier, quickly packed their bags and moved on. I didn't miss the sight of their plump brown bodies scurrying back and forth over the slabs by the bird feeders.

Every morning when she heard me she'd appear as if through a rent in the air between this world and the next, as if she'd been waiting just for the sound of my voice to summon her. And then she'd stay with me for as long as I was outside. Sometimes she followed me to the kitchen door, and she would have come right inside if I'd let her. Her days were spent shimmying between flower beds, graciously accepting her breakfast peanuts and her lunchtime sausages, sometimes eating the latter immediately but more often digging a shallow hole and burying them for later. For the lean times. Her supper snack of cheese and a bonio she tended to eat straight away, and then she'd slide back through the fence before dusk and the advent of the badgers, be gone until the next morning.

Once when we were out for the whole day my neighbour told me that the vixen had paced the garden for a couple of hours, waiting, and then she'd ascended the wooden steps to the sun terrace above the kitchen. She'd pawed at the door and windows, sprung onto the chairs, and possibly even considered picking a lock before finally retreating to the long grass at the top of the bank. All the time we'd been away I'd been fretting about her. Had she found the stash of sausages and the extra scoop of dog food I'd left by her favourite flower bed? Did she feel rejected by my absence? I missed her when I wasn't with her, eager to be home again.

Despite my infatuation I always resisted the temptation to lay my hand on the fur at the back of her neck and ruffle it through my fingers or trail a soft fingertip down the blaze of crisp white that ran the length of her narrow muzzle. I always put her food down on the ground between us, for her to take it from there and not directly from me. She was already seemingly half-tamed, bold and trusting, and though I longed to step over the tiny gap that was closing more every day, I couldn't do such damage to her. There might come a time when she wanted to pull away from me, from her state of semi-domesticity, and I couldn't bear the thought of the confusion she might feel about my role in her life, and about humans in general.

In July two kittens arrived and my home, which had been far less of a home without a cat, became whole again. But with their presence came a crushing anxiety. I remembered a news story from several years earlier about a fox that preyed on its neighbourhood cats, the vast stash of feline bodies and bones found around its den. And hadn't there once been a hysterical report in one of the tabloid newspapers about a fox entering a house and attacking a baby? What would I do when the kittens were old enough to go outside and explore the wider world, how would I keep them safe?

I was doing exactly what I'd condemned others for doing; I was demonising foxes. I'd had my flirtation with the wild and now I wanted to retreat behind the safe, high wall of the domestic, lock the doors and fasten the windows; turn my back on the creature who'd brought me such simple and profound happiness through the last couple of months when I was lonely and bereft, in need of animal company.

I worried constantly as the kittens grew and began to show an interest in exploring further than the confines of the house, watched idly through the glass of the back door by the fox as she waited for me to go outside. I layered my acute sense of responsibility for them over my sense of responsibility for the vixen, flailing beneath it all. I couldn't reject Miss Pumpkin now, not after the weeks spent encouraging her to view my garden as a place of safety. I couldn't stop feeding her now that I'd started.

She resolved the problem for me before I needed to confront a situation where both she and the cats would have to share outdoor space. She disappeared one day, as abruptly as she'd arrived. At first I thought that she'd merely changed her routine a little. I knew she also visited a neighbour at the far end of the terrace – by sheer accident I'd discovered that she popped by there for a daily snack – but when I spoke to my neighbour she told me that she'd not seen the vixen, either. She'd stopped visiting on the same day as I'd last seen her.

My first feeling was relief, then guilt for feeling relief. Then concern. I walked the lanes for a mile or so in every direction and I checked fields and hedges, walking fence lines, wincing at the thought of finding a body. It was late summer by this point, the days shortening and bumping sharply up against twilight hours that held the promise of a chilly night ahead. I waited for her to return, set the camera trap every evening to try and catch a glimpse of a nocturnal visit. There was no sign.

I have to think she'd finally grown into her wildness; a point of no return reached with the suddenness of a blink. Last year's cub at last feeling the tug of hormones and maturity. I have to think she left to strike out for territory of her own, to find a mate and start the rest of her life as an adult fox. The alternative is too distressing to contemplate.

The Bereft Sparrowhawk

The keening started one August day. The sound was pure desolation, pitched high to reach as far as possible. It was relentless, pursuing me whenever I went outside; sometimes rising to a shriek of anguish and sometimes fading to a mournful series of cheeps that were almost like quiet, choked sobs of despair. There would be silence for a moment and then it would start again. Day after day.

The smaller birds – the blackbirds and jackdaws, finches and sparrows – were at first agitated, furious, frightened. They took it in turns to mob the juvenile sparrowhawk, trying to dislodge it from its tree branch, but it barely noticed their presence and didn't even bother to flick a warning wing in their direction. Its sorrow was too vast, its sense of rejection too all-consuming, to have any care for anything else. And after a few days, with no distinct change of behaviour from the hawk, the smaller birds relaxed and continued with their own routines and essential pursuits, ignoring the bird of prey as if it were invisible to them. I wondered if they understood its cries and viewed it, in this vulnerable state, as the pathetic creature it currently was. No threat to them.

Once I'd located the sparrowhawk, it was easy to spot at a glance, perched on an outlying branch of the sycamore tree that stood at the end of my neighbour's garden. Now a young adult, turned out by its parents, all it wanted was to return to the safety and security of its natal nest, to the mother and father who'd nurtured and fed and brooded it. Once or twice a day it flew back to the small private woodland at the top of the hill behind the terrace – the site of the sparrowhawks' annual breeding ground – and then returned within an hour. It was presumably spurned by its weary but resolved parents or it discovered afresh an empty home and no dinner on the table.

For the week or so that it lasted, until the juvenile hawk realised that there would be no response, no rescue, I couldn't escape the sound of its distress. If I were indoors and the windows open, I could hear it wailing. And even when it stopped the sound was still there, pressed upon the air, pressed into my ears so that I thought I'd never be able to unhear it.

August is usually the quiet month for birds. They've survived another breeding season and are subdued, maybe moulting or just recuperating from the mammoth undertaking they've once more endured and survived. I was used to not really seeing or hearing anything of significance: all of us animals united to a greater or lesser degree in our preparation for the encroaching autumn; all of us inhabiting a quieter, more reflective mindset.

But this August, the sparrowhawk shattered the gentle melancholy of the late summer with its loud and demanding grief, breaking its heart over and over as publicly as possible until I was tearful myself, standing out in the garden and pleading with its parents to take pity and bring it a meal, or at the very least give it a few crumbs of comfort. Knowing they wouldn't, because of course they couldn't. Their job was done, and it had been done successfully. It was up to their offspring now to make or break its chance at negotiating this world.

It seemed to me as though its mourning, the extremity of its sorrow, was the voice of summer's death. The bird keened for all of those who were lost and lonely, scared to face a winter alone; not yet brave enough to know they can do it if they have to.

And not only do it but be stronger for it, because come next spring and an entire new year of birth and death and survival, the relentless, eternal wheel of life will all start again. And we'll all carry on.

Dawn Chorus

When the alarm sounded at 4.15am I was tempted to switch it off and roll over, bury my face in the pillow for another few hours. I'd lain awake until around two, unable to relax purely because I knew it was imperative that I fell asleep *right now* if I wanted to get through the next day relatively coherently. But this was the morning Si and I had decided would be our first, and probably last, dawn chorus experience. I heaved myself, light-headed and nauseous from exhaustion, downstairs to the kettle and a strong mug of coffee.

We took our second mug out onto the terrace and walked past the blank faces of our neighbours' houses – nobody awake but us – up to the small wood at the far end. Through the turnstile gate and into the damp, fragrant tunnel of trees. It was May but surprisingly cold, our hot coffee breath misting the air in front of us. A badger, ambling its way along the narrow earthen path towards home, stopped abruptly and slumped back on its haunches for a moment as it considered the threat. Then our human scent reached it and it turned and fled, disappearing into the undergrowth. I wondered if it was one of 'my' badgers.

When I'd mooted the idea of seeing in a dawn chorus to Si, he'd been tentatively agreeable, probably thinking my enthusiasm was more for the idea of it than reality. But here we were, in the middle of the thin strip of woodland that spooled between two lanes, in what was essentially still night. Stumbling over each other and hissing grumpily as we tried to find a suitable log to perch on.

I'd heard the dawn chorus plenty of times in the past, been

woken painfully early by the first harsh croaks of the crows clearing their throats on the roof, before the robins and blackbirds took over and then the wrens got their boxing gloves on and started swinging. But I'd been in bed then, dazed with tiredness, just wanting everything to pipe down so I could get back to sleep. My notions about a *proper* dawn chorus, one I've met head-on and deliberately, were all Snow White and her flitting cloud of bird friends, me and Si beaming at each other as the song around us reached some exquisite climax just as the sun burst over the horizon and drenched us all in a treacled warmth.

I hadn't considered the possibility of background noise. It wasn't even 5am and we live in a small rural village so passing traffic at this time would be rare to non-existent. But as we shuffled back and forth on a slimy, not quite big enough log, all we could hear was the steady, constant throb of machinery from the farm across the river. Somewhere in the vicinity of our garden the woodpigeons and crows woke up, in turn disturbing the jackdaws. Down by the moorings the estuary birds started stirring, calling to each other. I could make out the trembling flute of the curlew and the yapping, yodelling cries of the gulls. We decided to return home, where maybe the row of houses between us and the noisy farm would act as a muffler for the worst of its output.

So far, the dawn chorus experience wasn't going as planned.

I put the kettle back on and eyed the brandy thoughtfully, decided a slug of it in coffee before breakfast on a workday probably wasn't the wisest idea. I joined Si in the garden just as the wrens bowed out of threatening to fight everyone and the chaffinches started up. We sat side by side on the wooden steps that lead up to the sun terrace and watched the world around us thin and lighten into day.

Crow and Panda Bear appeared from the field at the back of the house; wild creatures in their night-time costumes, staring at us in horror. This was their time, not ours. We weren't supposed to be awake at this hour and monitoring whatever mischief they got up to. They shrugged past their chagrin and sidled over to join us, flirtingly domestic now and expectant of an early breakfast.

We wandered down to the moorings with our fourth coffee and a packet of biscuits. We sat on a bench overlooking the Teifi and watched as the peeping sun seared a sharp line of gold across the top of the hill opposite. A little while later, less shy now, a plump wedge of yellow clambered over the horizon and soaked into the fields that slid down to the banks of the river. We yawned and tucked our coats tightly around us, shivering but not wanting to leave until the sunrise was complete. Not realising until right now how long it all took.

The sun heaved itself fully into the sky as we drank our coffee and ate KitKats. It left the ground behind, a thin slice of faded blue beneath its burnt sails, and it was suddenly, properly morning. The river sparkled with light, and warmth rushed to touch us. A comfort. A blessing. We could go home now.

As I turned the key in the lock and let us back into our house – the working day with its usual routines and busyness lying ahead – I turned to Si and saw him smiling as widely as I knew I was. Tired but serene, the pair of us.

'That was lovely,' he said. 'Let's not do it again.'

'Maybe next year,' I said. 'But, no, maybe not.'

Beyond
THE GARDEN WALL

Winter Barn Owl over the Teifi Marshes

The winter had started early. Hard frosts in November laid a crust of ice over the world, freezing garden ponds and slicking the untreated roads with an unnatural black shine that swiped your legs out from under you if you didn't tread carefully. By the middle of December, the ground was as hard as a diamond, hedgerows and trees glittering with platinum streamers. The lane that threads through the steep Cwm Degwel valley and rarely sees winter sun was a spectacle of icicles that never thawed; the gardens around St Dogmaels strung with lace as the frozen cobwebs caught the sharp, pale light.

At the Teifi Marshes the pools and creeks froze over. The reedbeds, stiff and brittle, no longer rustled languidly in the wind but knocked together in a bristling, glassy way. When we walked there and saw the thick layers of ice over the ponds, the ducks and kingfishers and wading birds skating and swooping over it miserably, I worried for them all, wondered how they'd be able to catch the tiny fish and invertebrates they needed to survive.

My own garden birds were struggling despite the efforts I made to keep cleaning out and refreshing the water bath and bowls, topping up their food every few hours and regularly re-breaking the ice that filmed the water. The shy dog fox who usually slunk into the garden at dusk from the field behind the house was now appearing mid-morning to scavenge seed from the ground below the feeders, his thin body lending the only colour to the bleached scene.

When I walked the four-mile loop away from the village and

back again, as I still did as regularly as possible, I took small and careful steps along the lanes that I knew hadn't been treated or thawed by the sun, skidding at times and feeling that second of exhilarating freefall when your feet slide in opposite directions and there's nothing you can do to save yourself. Until my pinwheeling arms and trusty Doc Martens with their biting tread brought me back to a steady upright. My indrawn breath knifed my chest unless I wore a scarf wrapped around the lower part of my face to filter the cold out a little.

Every day there was a buzzard perched on one of the thigh-high posts by the side of the lane when I passed into the dark and frozen heart of the Cwm Degwel gorge. When it saw me it flew stiffly away in slow, jerking swoops, only a metre above the ground. It would come to a halt on a further post to glance back and then take to the air again, carrying on a little way more when it realised I was following. I always pitied it and felt guilty that I was flushing it from its perch, forcing it to expend precious energy it could ill afford to use. The ground had been so hard for so long, even its fallback diet of worms was unobtainable.

It would eventually, wearily, fly across the stream in a low glide and land on the steep bank there, watch and wait for me to pass. If this harsh winter continued for much longer I didn't see how it could possibly survive.

I'd heard from a few people that a barn owl had been seen over the Teifi Marshes, hunting in daylight. Forced by desperate need to abandon its usual nocturnal pattern, apparently it frequently appeared in the late afternoon, quartering the reed beds. Though I frequently saw and heard tawny owls around St Dogmaels it had been over a decade since I'd seen a barn owl, and that wasn't here in Wales but in Sussex where I'd lived for a few years with an ex-partner on a converted Bedford coach near Lurgashall, in the shadow of Blackdown Hill, where Tennyson once lived. Every evening a barn owl would appear from the woodland at the corner of the village green and flow along the pristine length of it, drifting towards and over us as it hunted.

I'd loved living in Sussex, despite the grim daily commute to work as a tenancy support officer in Guildford, and the hostility from wealthy local landowners who saw us and our unconventional home as undesirable. On summer evenings glow worms pricked through the grass around the coach in their dozens, lighting up the dusk like tiny, dropped lanterns – I'd never seen a glow worm before then and haven't seen one since – and green woodpeckers scattered the ground whenever I went outside, jeering and laughing noisily at me and each other. Herds of roe and fallow deer wandering past woke me early in the morning.

Now, I was torn between wanting to see the barn owl hunting over the Marshes and feeling stricken about why it was there in daylight hours. Hunger and necessity had forced it out of its roost before the extreme cold of the winter nights drove the rodents it needed for food back to their dens, pushing it into the dangerously overlapping territory of birds of prey like peregrines and goshawks. Fierce predators who wouldn't take kindly to sharing scarce pickings with an owl.

What was a wonderful photo opportunity for the many wildlife photographers who visit the Teifi Marshes, and a tick in the ledger for the twitchers, was a situation fraught with peril and the very real threat of injury or death for the owl. But certain death due to starvation sat on the other side of the scales and so its decision to hunt in the daytime wasn't really any kind of choice at all.

Si and I drove down there one afternoon during the final dark days of December. The cold weather and the wistful nostalgia that another year's end always summoned for me – the scanty list of things achieved set against the list of all the broken resolutions and sidelined intentions – seemed an appropriate backdrop to witness the fragile and wispy sight of a desperate and hungry barn owl.

We walked briskly along the main path that bisected the Marshes, striding through the dense huff of our frozen breath. We exchanged murmured salutes of *Merry Christmas* and *Happy New Year* with anyone we passed, had an amicable squabble about whether you could still say Merry Christmas after the day itself was behind you. The confusion most of us feel during this baggy, muddled, between-times week between Christmas Day itself and the new year had us firmly in its grip. I yawned as we walked, not sure how long I'd been awake or how long I'd be able to stay awake.

We decided not to go into the empty, iced hides that scattered along the path, loitered instead at a break between the parade of twisted blackthorn for a few moments, and then continued on. To the deserted, grey car park where we stood with our elbows on the fence and gazed out over the abandoned and somehow lifeless marsh. And then we turned and walked back up the path.

On this return journey we could see the distant bodies of fellow walkers, and when they got closer we could see that they hefted huge camera lenses. We all met at that natural gap between the otherwise unbroken avenue of blackthorn; the spot where people often gather to watch the starlings murmurate through the autumn as it offers long views in every direction.

As we exchanged greetings (we, and they, were there for the same reason) I eyed the shrivelled sloes drooping from the blackthorn around us, the pinched and frost-stricken fruit that had only a couple of months ago been plump and juicy. An essential ingredient for the gin I bottle annually. I guessed the berries must simply not have been considered by the birds to be nutritious or calorific enough while still in their pomp. That sharp shock of each grudging berry, without the sugar and the alcohol to tame and render it pleasurable, wasn't deemed worth the effort.

Our companions had been at this spot for the previous few afternoons with no luck, they told us; there had been no recent sightings of the hunting barn owl. I hoped it hadn't died of starvation already. We all stood around for a while making small talk, shuffling our feet to stay warm. I suddenly wanted to go home, to not be out here waiting for a famished wild creature to show itself, risking its life for a meal while the humans loitered to get their photograph and their *Oooh* moment. I turned to Si, about to suggest we start heading back to the car. But then I saw it. 'There,' I said, pointing across to the gnarl of trees on the other side of the path. Everyone swivelled round.

The barn owl flew over the 'kingfisher hide' and the swampy dip of marsh around it. Its gaze was steady and acute; totally measured and wholly emotionless in its assessment of the ground beneath it. It reached us and continued past without a flicker of acknowledgement, heading for the reed beds just ahead. I grasped Si's hand and watched as it flitted on silent snowy wings up and down the reed beds, hovering for a moment and then continuing on. There was something of the nightjar about it, about that gliding and fairy-like flight. The way both birds seem to float on the air without really moving their wings.

Cameras clicked around us. The owl hovered again, hung against the bitter winter sky like an ornament, and then it dropped down, out of sight into the reeds. Every part of me strained with the hope that it had caught something but when it rose back up its talons were empty. The anguish I felt for it then blurred my eyes and I tugged on Si's hand, jerked my head back towards Cardigan. The owl was moving away, quartering a different patch of the reed beds, and the photographers were standing in a huddle checking their cameras and comparing shots.

As we walked away, along the path towards the bypass bridge and Cardigan town, I looked back and saw the owl hover again, plunge again. This time when it arose there could have been something in its talons; a meal to make the risk of all this worthwhile. It was too far away to know for sure. I turned back to face home and told myself that it *had* caught something. It would eat and it would survive another day.

Hobbies at Cors Caron

Si had been to Tregaron Bog the weekend before with Sparky, and seen a hobby hunting over the pools. The sighting had been distant and brief, but exciting enough to make him want to change our plans for our Saturday outing and return there. I'd been holding out for a trip to the Dyfi Osprey Project, looking forward to seeing the osprey family in the flesh, so my acceptance of the altered programme for the day was grudging.

It was a hot June afternoon, and we were far later arriving in Tregaron than we'd intended. The air had gathered a sticky, sleepy humidity that drenched us when we got out of the car. Ours was the only vehicle in the car park; we were clearly the only two people stupid enough to venture out when the rest of the world, including the hobbies, would doubtless be dozing through the post-lunch hours until things cooled down.

We turned left out of the car park and walked along the raised boardwalk between swampy ponds, heading for the hide that overlooked a flat sweep of the wetland so that we could sit and eat our wilting, long-overdue sandwiches. I grumbled lightly, breathing in the heavy air, imagining how much pleasanter the observatory at the DOP would be, perched high above the heated ground and catching the breeze.

A bird of prey streaked overhead, low and fast; gone before we could raise our binoculars. 'Hobby!' Si called. But it was too big, too stocky. I'd never knowingly seen a hobby before but I'd seen enough photographs and video clips. After a bit of debate – wrong wing shape for a harrier; too small for a goshawk; too big for a kestrel – we decided it could only have been a peregrine.

Another bird of prey erupted up from the boardwalk ahead of us from where it had been resting on the wooden platform and flew away across the bog into the spiky line of pine trees. But as we watched it we could see that it wasn't a bird of prey, after all. This one I could now identify after my previous encounter with one of its kind: a female cuckoo.

'See,' Si said, pleased with himself, 'I told you coming here was a good choice.'

The boardwalk wound on between the ponds and streams, the air around us thick with dancing insects. There were dragonflies of every kind: hawkers and chasers scooting above the water; damselflies flitting like stained-glass suncatchers. Creeping plants trailed from the boughs of scarred trees and draped themselves over stunted, twisted shrubs. The scene, combined with the heat, summoned an image of Southern Gothic swampland. I'd have been terrified but not altogether surprised if an alligator had lifted its blunt snout from the muddy pool beside us to watch us pass.

The large hide, with its floor-to-ceiling windows and panoramic view of the bog, was a cool haven to settle in for a while and eat our late lunch. Directly in front of us, geese and ducks mingled with nearly a dozen herons and a couple of little egrets, all of them intent on foraging the wetland. Behind them the young Teifi flowed. We'd walked to its source, a couple of miles from this place, several years ago, and I'd been overcome with wonder and love as I'd stood straddled over the infant river. A mere trickle sliding between my boots, no wider than a hand span. Where I live in St Dogmaels, it's become an estuary, pouring itself into the sea as a vast and relentless giant.

After I'd rescued a bee that was pushing itself weakly against the hide window over and over, releasing it back outside and watching it fly away, we decided to return to the car park via the boardwalk and then strike out in the other direction, following the old railway line towards Ystrad Meurig. In our time in the hide there'd been no sightings of anything other than the geese and wading birds, and a red kite cruising overhead. Nothing I didn't already see daily at home. The gritty heat combined with a full stomach were sapping my energy levels. If we didn't move soon, I was going to fall asleep right where I sat.

We gathered our water bottles and binoculars and made our listless way back into the scorched afternoon.

Above our heads, just outside the entrance to the hide, two hobbies flew in lazy circles, low enough to be able to identify them immediately and without doubt. They really did look like large swifts. One twitched suddenly, catching a dragonfly and bringing it to its beak to eat on the wing. We followed them as they meandered away over the swampy pools, stopping whenever they were above us so that we could watch them properly as they hunted and weaved around each other. Through his binoculars, Si could make out the rusty trousers and striking dark moustache on each bird. He kept exclaiming excitedly, urging me to use my own binoculars to get the kind of close views he was getting, but I didn't need that sense of clarity that he craved. I preferred a more organic and less removed experience; without that crispness of focus perhaps, but more intimate, with nothing imposed between me and the creatures I was watching.

There was a third hobby in the distance, flying nearer to us as we continued walking. It joined the two that were already circling and they all feasted on dragonflies for a few minutes, keeping a distance from each other but seemingly not bothered by the others' presence. I supposed that there was such a glut of insects, they could afford to be tolerant and not guard the territory too fiercely.

All three drifted away and out of sight, and we returned to the car park. Re-energised now, full of enthusiasm, we struck out in the opposite direction and began to walk the path that ran parallel with the road and gave wide, long views of the bog at our side.

We used to walk this path years ago when we heard about the golden eagle who lived in the Tregaron area for a decade or so. A captive-bred bird, she'd escaped when still young enough to learn wildness and she'd made the hills of mid Wales her home. Over a couple of years we returned again and again, through all the seasons, to try and spot her, but never managed to. And then the news broke that she'd died, her body found in a stream by a walker.

Though the views to our left were stunning, albeit in a desolate and forbidding way, the constant noise from the road and the glimpses of the hurtling cars on our right were unpleasant and distracting. Tiredness settled on us again, the heat swimming up from the path making me slightly dizzy. I longed to fast-forward the walk back to the car and the long drive ahead, be instantly home and in my garden under the shade of the hawthorn.

But then a raucous clamour started up, high in a thick stand of pine trees on the verge of the road. I assumed it was a raven's nest – I'd stood beneath one in Cwm Gwaun once and marvelled at the tumult one nest of corvid chicks could create – and called out to Si to stop for a moment. The noise was tremendous, a harsh and layered shrieking that drilled through the spongy air, tearing it apart. Beside it there was another eruption. More strident screeching. I backed up and craned to look but couldn't see more than the twiggy, messy bottom of the huge nests.

Above my head a heron appeared. It glided silently into the tree in front of me, followed a few seconds later by another heron. Beak sloppy with fish, this one flew into the tree beside it. The shrieking was now replaced by a fury of hollow clapping sounds and frantic gobbling, more like desperate choking. I'd stumbled across my first ever heronry.

Though I couldn't see the chicks feeding I remembered the *Springwatch* footage I'd watched a couple of years before, so I could visualise what was happening above me. A siege of young herons would be clashing their beaks together, fastening them tightly over the parent's beak to be first to receive the regurgitated meal. Pecking and shoving their siblings out of the way; pale eyes bulging, cold and fixed as pebbles. The scene is barbaric, brutal, and quite repulsive; wild creatures behaving true to themselves.

There's nothing cute or pretty about young herons past the fluffy stage. Gangly and prehistoric looking, they've yet to find the austere, brooding grace of adult birds. All legs and beak, and wild Mohican hairdo topping a face whose expression is one of permanent outrage and shock. I wondered how many chicks were in each nest, and whether there were any others in the trees beside them. Heronries can hold as many as a dozen or more separate nests so it was likely that this stand of trees was sheltering a number of them. I'd been surprised to see so many herons foraging on the bog in front of the hide earlier, and now I knew why they'd been sharing such close space.

First one heron and then another left their nest and glided out from the trees, over my head and back to the pools to gather another meal. The chicks immediately fell silent, no doubt watching the adults fly away. From their vantage point, they'd be

able to see the return flight and then the screeching would start again, the beak-clashing: calling their parents home.

Swifts at the Watch House

Of all the reasons to love spending summer evenings at the Ferry Inn – sitting outside on the decking and watching the waters of the Teifi slide past; counting the number of shelduck chicks in one creche; watching the curlews and oyster catchers newly returned from their breeding quarters – the swifts that hurtle and shriek around the hodgepodge building with its layers of different storeys and protruding extensions are at the very top of my list. That first sight and sound of one of them at the start of May is greeted with joy and relief. So this won't be the awful, silent year when there are no longer any swifts left to make the migration and come home to raise their chicks. There is still time for humans to turn things around.

A couple arrive first, plunging over the lane and gardens between my home and the river, then another couple appear a few days later. Maybe several more, a week after that. By June, the numbers have swollen to a small flock, about a dozen. Far, far fewer than we used to get when I first moved here years ago; every one of them a treasure to cherish.

Now on the red list and in real danger of becoming extinct in my lifetime, the swift population has crashed over the last twenty or so years. I've read reports that we've lost as many as 70% of these beautiful birds since the 1990s, due to the usual mix of loss of nesting habitat and overuse of pesticides. As the adults don't land on the ground – eating, mating, sleeping on the wing – each bird needs to catch as many as a hundred thousand flying insects a day when they're feeding young.

A hundred thousand a *day*. That figure is so vast I find it difficult to fully comprehend it.

I used to assume they nested somewhere in the eaves of The Ferry, as fond as they are of zooming around the elongated building in tight, fast loops, hour after hour. When June gives way to July and the fledglings and screaming parties of prospecting youngsters join the throng, the numbers swell to twenty and more. For a few weeks, before they all depart for Africa and empty the sky of their sharp, precise flight and wonderful sound, the spectacle – sitting beneath them as they squeal and blast past, over and over – is magical.

Walking the perimeter of the pub looking for likely nest sites yielded nothing. I knew they had to be nesting close by, and so one evening I took my drink and left my seat on the decking. I walked out onto the lane that leads to Poppit Sands and stood outside the neighbouring property, the Watch House. Now a holiday home, as so many houses in St Dogmaels have become, this smartly refurbished building had two very new and shiny Range Rovers parked on its narrow drive. A little concerned that it might look like my interest lay in the vehicles, I hovered in the entrance to the driveway and schooled my features to innocence.

The swifts careened into view in a screaming flock, grazing the sides of the building with their wingtips and arrowing up and over the roof a split second before it looked as though they were going to crash straight into it. I could hear them as they zip-wired around to The Ferry to complete their circuit of that building, and then they were back. Another high-speed loop of the Watch House and then most of them disappeared again, trailing the echo of their shrieks. But two peeled off from the group and flung themselves at the high front wall of the holiday home.

As I watched they hit the wall like Velcro toys, clung to the stone and then crawled up and under the wood fascia.

After a couple of minutes, first one and then the other reappeared, threw themselves from the tight crevices that housed their chicks and dropped like stones towards the ground. They came out of their dives a metre above the gravel, full throttle now and climbing steeply; up, up, clearing the roof and plunging out of sight.

On the next circuit another swift separated from the flock and threw itself at the wall of the Watch House, clambered deftly up the last inches and crawled into its nest. I could hear the eager chirps of the chicks as they greeted their parent and the meal it held in its cheek pouches. When this adult threw itself from the nest it skimmed the roof of the nearest Range Rover before rising in a steep arc and flying away. I really hoped the holiday home would never have a high-sided van parked on its driveway during the summer months.

I have a swift box on the front of my home, secured just under the jut of the roof. I worried when a kindly neighbour installed it, fretting that it wasn't high enough. I worried that passing cars on the terrace would plough into one of the birds as they plummeted down from the box to the ground, killing them in that moment before the strength of their wings and the strength of their spirit bore them back up into the sky. But watching these swifts at the Watch House negotiating the changing terrain of their historic nesting site, assessing the different levels of danger and folding those dangers into their flight patterns and their feeding routines, I thought my box would be perfect for any needy swifts. If only the house sparrows would move out for long enough for something else to move in.

Now that I know where the swifts are nesting, I can keep an eye on them every year, linger in the lane in the evenings to watch their comings and goings. I can note when they return and how many there are; how many leave at the end of the season. And if I see any damaging changes being made to the exterior of the building, I can find out who the owners are and appeal to them. For the loss of these birds to the village, the loss to me, would be vast. The thought of a future without swifts, the summer skies above The Ferry silent, doesn't bear thinking about.

Racing Swans on the Teifi

For four seasons, I was part of the St Dogmaels rowing team and rowed a Celtic longboat on the river and coast. Twice a week from April through to October we took to the water and pitted our small vessel against the push and shove of currents and waves. As a child, I'd been told I wasn't sporty, I had no co-ordination, and so I was as surprised as anyone when I climbed tentatively into the boat one summer day for a trial row and discovered that *this* I could do, and do naturally and well.

I loved everything about rowing. I loved the essential rhythm and repetition of it; the intimate camaraderie with people I otherwise had no daily connection to; the way the exercise revealed and honed muscles I hadn't even known I had. Most of all, I loved the feeling when I took my place in the boat, strapped my feet and grasped the oar – I was usually on stroke to set the pace for the rest of the team – and was able, for the entire time I was out on the water, to unplug myself and my busy anxious mind from conscious thought and channel it into something bigger and calmer. I was part of a machine when we were rowing, and I couldn't detach myself from that wider body without endangering the people around me. It was the closest I've ever been to true peace, a blank serenity I imagine other people achieve through meditation or yoga.

We rowed the Teifi more often than not. Launching from the moorings and making our way through the village and beyond, towards Cardigan town and under the two bridges that bookended it. On a high tide we could get as far as the deep, shadowy gorge below Cilgerran Castle. On autumn nights we'd return to St Dogmaels as dusk gathered, the lights of the houses against the hillside glittering like fairy lights ahead of us as we neared the village.

Sometimes we'd launch the longboat from Poppit Sands and row out of the bay and around Cardigan Island. Those longer, physically exhausting sessions were less enjoyable for me: the waters around the island are fast and treacherous, the surface of the sea running like rapids as it's funnelled between the island and the mainland. On stroke, I couldn't miss a beat; my arms worked like steady pistons and my focus was fixed entirely, unblinkingly, on the cox as they bellowed us round the choppy, rocky route and into safer waters.

We'd stop sometimes, safely back in the bay and half a mile from shore, to rest and chat, smoke a cigarette or even drop a fishing rod over the side. A seal would occasionally appear beside us and watch us intently, dark eyes full of curiosity. Once, two dolphins breached close by, rolling lazily over the surface of the sea and creating a wave that rocked our little boat. Everyone was filled with excitement at the sight of them and I'd pretended to join in but hadn't managed to get myself past the instinctive fear of a creature far bigger than I was, bossing us in its natural environment. I can swim, but the beach was a long way away and I doubted I could swim that far if the dolphins decided to give us a playful nudge and tip us overboard.

We capsized one evening, caught by a sudden fierce wave as we came into shore. It knocked us sideways and then the next wave flipped the boat as we were trying to straighten out, flinging us overboard. We were close enough to the beach to only be a little out of our depth and though it was frightening there was no harm done. Other than to me and my mental health.

The next time we took to the sea I had an anxiety attack that left me weak and shaking, limbs boneless. I had to gather strength before I could grip the oar and row again. Nobody knew how badly I was struggling, I said I had a stitch, but I saw the quizzical look the cox gave me afterwards and when he asked me outright what the problem was, I told him.

He was supportive, sympathetic, and we tried twice more to row at sea under his careful guidance. But the panic – brutal, savage, hijacking me from nowhere – didn't stop. I decided then that I would only row the river from now on. I couldn't be responsible for the potential danger I was placing the rest of the team in, if the anxiety hit me.

After a couple of weeks, the same panic caught and held me when we rowed the Teifi. I'd lost faith in myself and any ability I had by then; from the moment I got in the boat I was anticipating the surge of anxiety, braced for it to snatch my strength and reduce me to a state of hyperventilating helplessness. I'd forgotten what it was that I'd ever loved about rowing, my mortification and self-loathing ruining any pleasure or peace I might find in the thought of being back on the water. That constant watchfulness was exhausting in itself, waiting for the cruelly inevitable anxiety to unfold from the pit of my stomach and flood me. By the end of that season, I'd stopped rowing altogether.

A year later when I went on a riverboat that chugged lazily from Cardigan to Poppit and back, it took every ounce of self-control to stay seated with the other passengers and appear calm. Every part of me was shrilling with the compulsion to climb overboard and leap for the bank that slid slowly past us. When we docked, I was too weak to walk and had to sit on the quayside in

Cardigan until I'd regained the strength and composure needed to be able to stand.

I haven't been back in a boat since then, and I don't know if I ever will. I can't bridge the oceans' deep gap between the strong, eager woman who rowed all the way out to Cardigan Island and around it, and the woman I am now. Sometimes I'll pass the moorings and watch the current team launching the longboat, chatting happily as they set their feet and lift their oars, push out from the shore. The disconnect between the person who once took her seat in the stern and closed her eyes, became a vital part of something bigger than herself, and this land-bound person, is total. I have to turn and walk away.

But at other times the physical memory of the rhythm of the row, the weight of the oar in my hands and the tugging of muscles in my stomach, sets up a yearning and a profound sense of loss that brings tears to my eyes and keeps me close to watch them as they raise their oars in unison and pause for a moment before they begin to stroke away from me, past the jangle of fishing boats and small yachts that scatter this stretch of the river, heading for the beach or the town.

The world looks different from the water. No matter how many times we rowed past the Graig and the green, I could never stop marvelling at how St Dogmaels, a village I've lived in for years and know intimately, was made a beautiful stranger. It wasn't just the changed view, it was the changed mental perspective. When we came back to shore after a row and I took my first steps away from the boat, there was a moment of unfamiliarity. A strange, almost shy return to *this* person who walked *these* lanes, leaving behind my other self when I stripped off my lifejacket.

We knew the bend in the river, not visible from land, where

the kingfisher always perched on the slumped and intricate fretwork of a dead tree and watched us pass; we always slowed and looked out for it. When the shelducks flowed past, with their tangled line of chicks, we counted the bobbing heads to see how many of the tiny creatures had survived since the last row. Deep in the ancient wilderness of the Cilgerran gorge, where the cold slate banks rose steeply around us, the river below us deep and still, the sky above us lost beyond the overhanging trees, I began to write stories of monsters and desperate infatuation in my head that I then continued on paper when I got home.

The pair of mute swans who live on this stretch of the Teifi would glance at us coldly as we rowed past them, sometimes hissing and darting a warning beak if they had signets to protect but otherwise ignoring us as inferior things not worthy of their full attention.

Apart from the time one of them decided to show us just how gracefully, how swiftly and how easily a creature who truly belongs to the river can move.

We pull away from the moorings and slide past The Ferry, nodding and smiling at the punters who wave at us from the decking. Past the first big bend in the river and the vast oak that guards it. No perching kingfisher today as we row beneath the Graig path. Though I'm facing away and can only see the world streaming past in reverse, I know that at any moment the outlying buildings of Cardigan town will appear distantly over my shoulder and then we'll soon be carefully negotiating the arches of Cardigan bridge

before the river flattens and spreads as we draw level with the Teifi Marshes.

The swan, as we pass it, sneers slightly but doesn't otherwise react. The river is tougher this evening, the tide and currents against us. Sweat is already slick on my body, the late-summer air heavy around me. I slacken the stroke slightly, just enough to give us all a moment to slow the pace a little, gather ourselves before the hard push through the turbulent whirlpooling thrust of the river beneath the bridge. I watch the swan as it watches us, gliding gently in the wash of the boat.

And then it twitches as if shocked, rears up from the water's surface and spreads its wings. It begins to run after us, huge black feet pounding the surface of the Teifi. It races towards the boat, tucks its webbed feet up into the velvet plush of its stomach and takes flight.

Galvanised now, in competition, we all pick up the pace as the bird beats those vast wings, a foot above the river, and gains on us effortlessly. Shouting, laughing, we row faster, the cox calling to us to keep at it. And for a moment the swan is level with us, hanging in the air beside the boat, close enough to touch. The sound of its slow and easy flight fills the evening. It doesn't turn its head but I am sure it gives us a glint of contemptuous side-eye as we battle neck and neck for a couple of seconds. And then it pulls ahead, as it was always going to do, and lifts itself higher and leaves us behind.

We slow and rest our oars in the rowlocks, twist in our seats to watch the creature as it cruises along the river to join its mate, settling itself in the shallow water beside the bank with a flourish of wingbeats, hissing its triumph. Still laughing, joyful, we turn back to face the cox and begin to row in earnest as the swirling *currents around Cardigan's old bridge catch us. The swans slide past my gaze, their heads turned dismissively away from the sight of us. I keep my eyes fixed on them as we fight the Teifi's high-tide whirlpool waters that funnel under the narrow stone arches and spit us out on the other side of the bridge.*

Even after we've rowed beneath the bypass bridge and on to Cilgerran Gorge I keep my focus fixed on the river far behind the boat, half expecting to see the swan again. Hoping it will reappear for another race, give us a generous head start and then raise itself gracefully onto its feet, stir those huge wings and start running, annihilate our feeble human efforts.

Murmurating Starlings over the Teifi Marshes

I was late collecting the visiting poet from Carmarthen train station, coaxing my old car along the thirty-mile stretch of country roads and hoping the train would be delayed so he wouldn't have to wait long. Every month at the Cellar Bards, the spoken-word group in Cardigan that I used to host and manage, we had a guest writer. If they weren't local, it was my responsibility to ensure they got to and from the venue and had a place to stay for the night.

As an introvert, this part of my role was always one I met with a degree of trepidation. The poets were often total strangers, sometimes as shy and uncomfortable as I was with the situation. After much practise, I could now manage the hosting well, donning a social mask and compering each event as though these things came naturally to me, but the enforced sharing of domestic space was harder on both me and the guest. I'd worry about whether we would have a natural affinity that lifted us past the initial awkwardness, whether they'd like the food I'd cooked for dinner, whether they'd object to my old tabby cat Hobbit making a fuss of them and climbing into their lap. Luckily, most of these visiting poets arrived as strangers but left as friends.

On the way home from Carmarthen, making careful small talk as we headed back to St Dogmaels, I suddenly asked this month's guest writer if he'd like to take a brief detour to the Teifi Marshes to watch the starlings murmurate over the reed beds. It was a tentative ice breaker and one I thought would appeal to him, having read his wonderful nature-infused poetry. We were deep into November; the starlings would by now be gathering in their thousands. I figured the diversion would at least take care of that difficult hour before preparing dinner and heading to the venue, when he was adrift in a stranger's home.

We arrived at the reserve's car park with time to spare. The sun was low in the sky, the horizon swollen with streaks of peach and indigo, but the starlings hadn't yet arrived. I led the way along the narrow, twisty path that threaded behind the wildlife centre, the scenic route to the high grassy plateau by the huge wicker badger that would give us the best views of any murmurating birds.

In motion now, freed from having to make self-conscious conversation whilst static in the car, I was exuberant and chatty, leaping ahead. We took a wrong turn and then another, eventually arriving at the river where we had to turn around and retrace our steps. The gathering twilight and my own nervousness made everything look unfamiliar and though I could see the domed body of the wicker badger in the distance, looming above us, I couldn't work out how to reach it without walking back to the car park and striking out again along the more direct path. We ended up climbing the bank and wading uphill through thigh-high bracken to reach the grassed area. I was breathlessly apologetic and he was breathlessly gracious, reassuring me that this was a perfect way to spend the winter afternoon.

We stood together, shy and awkward again, reduced to the minutiae of small talk once more as we waited for the starlings. There were a few small huddles of people around us, some with cameras. I recognised a few people and exchanged hellos, shuffled back and forth to stay warm. I hadn't brought a coat; my decision to divert us from the usual route home hadn't been planned.

In the distance, over the old town bridge, a small dark cloud floated like a scrap of wool in the otherwise clear, glassy sky. I squinted and pointed. 'I think that's a flock heading over.'

As we watched, the cloud got bigger and closer. I spun in a slow circle to scan the horizon all around us. There was another, much bigger, flock flowing from the direction of Cilgerran, and another arriving from the area north of Cardigan. We both pointed – 'There!' 'And there!' – as flock after flock of starlings surged with concentrated single-mindedness towards the safety of the reed beds that spread themselves below us. They rushed towards each other with the urgency of reunited lovers, one group absorbing another and then another; swelling to fill half the sky.

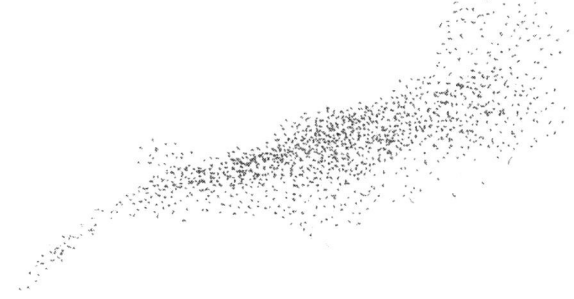

They all seemed to slow in their flight once they'd tucked themselves into the more secure embrace of a single vast flock; no longer frantic. Above our heads they spun and rolled, concertinaing, unfolding and refolding like a painted paper fan spread open and then closed over and over. A zoetrope set in motion and spilling endless patterns across the huge dusk sky. The sound of thousands of beating wings replaced all other sound, filled my ears with a constant silky rustling so that I could almost imagine feathers sprouting through the loose fall of my hair. I glanced at my companion, exchanged a grin of pure delight, and then tipped my head back to watch the birds again.

The fringes of the flock broke away and began to pour themselves down into the reed beds: the signal to the rest that the murmuration was over. Their bodies cascaded like liquid into the reeds, hundreds at a time, emptying the sky. And once they were all on the ground, the high, raucous sound of their squabbling, gossiping conversation reached us. Now simply birds again, no longer magical creatures, they bustled and settled deep in the wetland, lost amongst the vegetation.

As we walked back to the car, we were drunk with the joy of what we'd seen; our ears still filled with the sound of the starlings' flight, our vision still patchworked with the sight of them. And that shift between us, from stranger to friend, had been as seamless and fluid as the murmuration.

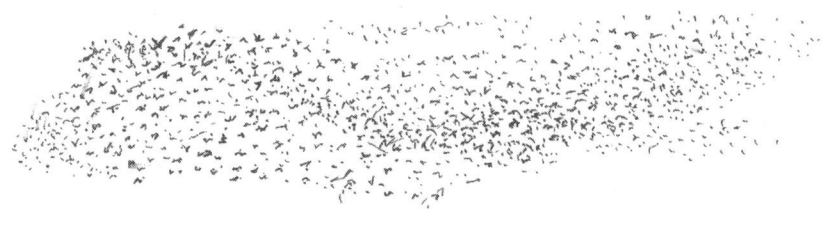

Crossbills at Pantmaenog Forest

Our neighbours told us about the crossbills at Pantmaenog, the forest a mile or two from Rosebush in Pembrokeshire. 'We didn't need to get out of the car,' they said. 'We just parked up in the car park and there they were. Two of them, sitting in the trees next to us.'

I'd never seen a crossbill, so Si and I decided to head down there for a walk. It was autumn, a cool, drizzly and uninviting Sunday afternoon. But if the weather got worse it didn't sound as if we'd even have to get out of the car to see the birds if we didn't want to.

I wondered what it was about car parks at nature reserves or rural woodland sites that seemed to attract birdlife. After our nightjar experience at Cross Inn Forest – back at the car, after a three-hour walk to find them had been declared a failure – I was full of optimism that just parking up at Pantmaenog and switching off the ignition would summon the crossbills. And if that didn't work then switching the engine back on and preparing to go surely would.

After we'd sat in the car for twenty minutes, peering through the misted windows into the bleak, greyed day, we decided grudgingly to get out and venture along the trails that carved through the plantation. My optimism had faded somewhat and I was already looking forward to getting home and opening a bottle of wine to ward off the gloomy Sunday Blues and gloomier Sunday weather.

Pantmaenog is a privately owned plantation of mainly coniferous trees within the Pembrokeshire Coast National Park.

Historically, the trees were grown and managed for the wood they provided, and though their existence is a good thing for crossbills it doesn't really allow for much in the way of a wider biodiversity for wildlife. There was a barren feel to the place as we trudged along the wide gravelled path, passing dark little pools of standing water and marshy tussocks of grass, greeting every corner-of-the-eye wing flutter hopefully. Dog walkers passed us, zipped to the chin in raincoats, nodding grimly.

We reached a T-junction and turned left, wandered along another wide path that rose up above the trees and gave us a more panoramic view of the wider landscape. But it was hard to make out anything in the lowering gloom and early dusk. A group of horse riders plodded past, and then a few sodden cyclists flew by with their bare legs caked in mud and their eyes fixed glaringly on the track ahead. Gravel spat from their bicycle wheels. We trudged on.

The rain started to gather spite, and when Si suggested we turn back and go home I didn't protest. I'm a fair-weather bird watcher and this wasn't fair weather.

It was obviously the wrong time of year, or the wrong time of day, we agreed as we drove home. Even if they were there, we wouldn't have been able to make them out through the murk of the dismal afternoon. Next time, though, we'd see them.

The pinecones were plump and ripe now on the trees, strung like apples from every branch. It was mid-summer, hot, and we'd decided to have another stab at looking for the crossbills.

This decision had been largely influenced by my neighbours – the same neighbours who'd been at Pantmaenog for a walk the previous weekend and told me they'd seen too many to count, flitting up high among the treetops, hanging from the juicy cones, calling to each other.

We collected Sparky en route and drove out to the forest. It hadn't rained for a couple of weeks and the air was heavy with pollen and a static, lazy heat. Hard to summon the energy to stride at my usual pace so I kept to Sparky's slow amble, swiping sweat from my forehead as he stood and stared through his binoculars at every bird we passed.

'Bluetit,' I'd say. 'It's a bluetit.'

'Bluetit,' he'd confirm with a nod and a sweet smile.

But we weren't there for the bluetits, we were there for the crossbills that had apparently flocked in thick clouds over the treetops only a week before. And apart from the occasional bluetit, or a warbler darting elusively through the high branches of a tree, there really was nothing else to see. Even other humans had decided not to venture out into the blazing afternoon.

A sudden brief rain shower, sharply refreshing, drove us into the shelter of the huge conifer trees, crouched among their roots on deep cushions of needles the colour of roasted almonds. The smell in our makeshift refuge was delicately spicy with a hint of pine air freshener gone stale, reminiscent of the old-fashioned cardboard trees you used to hang in a car and leave dangling for months.

Above our heads, dozens of birds chattered and flitted, deep among the maze of branches. So that's where the buggers were hiding. We couldn't see them through the dense foliage, and when the rain stopped and we were upright again on the track, viewing the trees from the outside, they were still invisible, even with binoculars. Every couple of minutes one of us would freeze.

'Oh! There's one. Crossbill!'

'No, that's a pinecone.'

'Ah, okay. I'm pretty sure there's one on the branch next to it though. It's very red.'

'No. that's a pinecone as well.'

On the way back to the car, we stopped to let a shrew scuttle right in front of us, in drunkenly haphazard zigzags, from one bank to another. A little later, a vole crawled weakly across the path. I wrapped it in a tissue and moved it to the undergrowth, off the hot and lightly steaming gravel, but it didn't look healthy and I doubted it would survive. There was another vole, this one dead, lying on the short incline just before the car park. It was odd to see so many rodents on one shortish walk in the middle of the day, and none of them well. I was sure the dead one hadn't been there at the start of the walk or I would have noticed it.

We hung around the car park for a while before heading home but no crossbills obliged by putting in a last-minute appearance. It was clearly the wrong time of year again, or the wrong time of day.

Either that or my neighbours had an interesting sense of humour.

Spring now, and another Sunday afternoon. Si and I were once more at Pantmaenog, following the 'third time lucky' philosophy of birdwatching. The air was cool and the breeze brisk, but the sun was out and we were buoyantly optimistic. Again.

The young cones on the trees we passed as we began to stride along the track were tender and green, glowing in the rinsed spring light. Dog walkers and Sunday strollers were out in force, including a couple with four very cute Pembrokeshire Corgis, all of whom required a fuss before we could continue on our way.

We'd covered two seasons, I thought, and were on our third. Spring and winter were the only ones left, and winter we'd save for last. I couldn't imagine this bleak landscape would be an inviting place in the dark end-months of the year so maybe, if we didn't hit gold today, we'd give any further pursuit of crossbills a miss. Unless, that is, my neighbours came round with a tantalising story of having seen a few hundred of them performing some obscure and intricate dance routine *right in the car park*.

Of course, there wasn't even a glimpse of a bird – any bird – for the entire length of the track. At the T-junction we turned right instead of left and wandered along there. Quarried slate heaped in small, slippery mountains at our sides, the coniferous plantation falling away to a different scene of scrubby little trees and lichen-splotched rock; the sky pale and wide above us. The landscape was alien, cold and grey and stark. Twisted, leafless shrubs reared up and fell behind as we walked.

Suddenly we were in a farmyard. There was a public right of way through it, we weren't trespassing, but my childhood memories of Pontsian farmyards always involved spiteful collies who couldn't be reasoned with. Nervous now, wondering whether we should just turn back, we tiptoed on, towards the Tafarn Sinc pub in Rosebush that we sensed was only a few hundred metres away. A pint right now would be bliss.

And then there was a gaggle of geese. They charged us,

necks stiffly horizontal, yellow beaks gaped wide and bubblegum tongues gleaming with rows of sharp tomia as they hissed their furious displeasure. But geese I'm comfortable with, my calm response to their bluff and swaggering intimidation a deep memory swimming up from thirty-plus years of once loving one of them.

When I was a child, I was the accidental wife of a blind gander. I'd called him Beep Beep, after the sound I made to guide him around, and cuddled and hand fed him when he was a fluffy yellow gosling. He followed me everywhere, squatting on my feet under the kitchen table at mealtimes and sleeping in my lap. And then he grew up, his hormones raging. He'd chase me around the garden, desperate to mate with me, incandescent with need and anger as soon as he heard my voice. Charging at me with a screech and gripping my trousers with his beak while he tried to wind his body around my leg. Often tripping us both up as he pressed his undercarriage furiously against my shins.

We got him a more appropriate wife then, a sweet-natured chocolate-brown goose called Delta who was endlessly patient with his tempers and his desires. She took over my role, fussed around him and guided him about the garden and put up with his general crankiness with a saintly serenity for several years, until he died suddenly. We found him one morning in the tin shed where he slept with Delta and the ducks; head tucked under his wing. Cold and stiff and finally silent. We buried him under the poplar trees and Delta – after a cursory mourning period – tagged onto the waddle of Muscovy ducks, seemingly content to spend her time with Sir Francis and his wives.

As the geese surrounded us here, barging in to drill at our ankles, I waded slowly through the flock without pausing, pulling a nervous Si along beside me. 'They're fine,' I told him. 'More bluster than anything else. Just keep walking.'

Once our backs were turned they gave chase, trying to force a panicked run from us. One particularly obstreperous bird hung onto a beakful of my coat and let me tow it along for a few steps before it let go and pecked frantically at my calf instead. If he got too feisty I'd have to stop and face him, hold his neck in a loose grip and turn him away, as I used to do with Beep Beep. But the pecking wasn't really that bad; those sharp-looking teeth aren't really teeth and aren't actually that sharp. And the hollow clap as their beaks snapped shut was a satisfying sound. A familiar sound.

We reached the gate and slid through, leaning our arms on the top rung for a moment to watch them as they milled about aimlessly, honking to each other. And then they waddled off, their animosity forgotten. I felt a sudden bitter spasm of sorrow, of nostalgia, remembering Beep Beep and Delta.

Tafarn Sinc was open and we sat outside in the beer garden for an hour – our first outdoor drink of the year – in the valiant spring sunshine, before deciding to walk back to the car by a different route, one that didn't cross through the farmyard. Si wasn't impressed by my wistful suggestions to maybe get a goose or two for the garden, and he hadn't been impressed by the pecking his ankles got. I knew no amount of reassurance would convince him that geese could ever become sweet-natured domestic pets.

But then, he'd never met Delta.

To this day, I have yet to see a crossbill.
I'm starting to doubt they exist.

Afterword

This book of encounters, and missed encounters, with nature around the Teifi valley started life over a decade ago as something very different. In its original incarnation, *Love Letters on the River* was a handful of page-long 'letters' – *literal* love letters – written to a fictional other; an unnamed person whose absence was as much a part of the fabric of the letters as were the birds in my garden that I was describing. My first novel had just been published and the themes running through that, and through a lot of my short stories, dealt with loss and yearning, absence as an active presence that we circle and can't release.

I wanted to write about the badgers that visited my garden, and about the racing swans, and Runty the jackdaw, but I wasn't yet confident enough to think I could attempt a book of nonfiction. I wrote stories, I made stuff up; that was how I explored the world around me. I needed the safety net of a genre I could move comfortably within. A genre that I could also hide within.

Wales Arts Review published a few of the *Love Letters* several years ago, and I was invited to the Caught by the River festival in 2015, where I read out a couple of them as part of a nature-writing panel. And then I abandoned the project and returned to purely writing fiction. Though it had been an interesting concept, there was too much room for the heart of it to become messy and confused. Was this hybrid book to be about my love for wild creatures or my yearning for a person who'd left me? The drama of the love affair, the questions raised – who is this person? What is their shared history? Will reconciliation ever be achieved?

– would, I think, have taken over the narrative and left a reader unsure of the point and the purpose of the writing itself. And of course it is the creatures themselves who should, rightly, be the stars of the show.

There are touches of that earlier writing in this incarnation, a sentence here or there that made the leap across the years: a brief description of the long-tailed tits in their glitzy outfits flitting around the feeders; the joyful race with the swan. So, in a way, this book is part of the same thread I started a decade ago, finally finished.

Rich and Gill from Parthian approached me a couple of years ago and mooted the idea of me writing a nature memoir. I'd just finished writing my second novel and was on the cusp of negotiating a publishing contract for it; the next year was going to be busy. I tentatively agreed to draft something over the following months, and I began making notes on different chapters. Then, a couple of weeks after that conversation, a juvenile osprey flew into my life and landed on a tree opposite the Ferry Inn, and I fell in love. Her chapter was the first one I wrote, almost in real time.

The other chapters span years but are mainly clustered around the last two or three. There are chapters I made notes on but then never actually wrote. What to include and what to leave out? The just-fledged female blackbird who couldn't yet fly, the apple of her devoted father's eye, who died at the beak of a magpie on the ground below the bird feeders while he flew repeatedly and desperately at it and screamed his distress as I ran towards them, too late to save her. Coming across a sparrowhawk perched atop the bank in the garden, eating a scrap of goldfinch, and having to lunge frantically to scoop up my cat Panda Bear who'd also seen it and fancied his chances, diving past me on his three legs to pounce.

Memory has played a huge part in writing this book. Not the faulty, creative kind of memory that's stored when things happen to us as we travel through life, but the immediate and intense well of *sense* memory. I only need to stare out of the window into the back garden to be able to summon the ghost sight and smell of the young vixen slinking through the fence and trotting down the path towards me. I can hear the nightjar's churring now when I close my eyes, and It still raises goose pimples on my arms. The sound of a wren alarm-calling brings me to my feet in a rush of panic, stomach lurching with anxiety.

It's given me a pure and profound pleasure to remember all of the encounters I've had with the creatures around me, and writing this has been a joy.

ACKNOWLEDGEMENTS

Thanks, firstly, to Rich and Gill for commissioning me to write this, and to Gwen and all at Team Parthian for the work that's done behind the scenes to turn a manuscript into a finished book. Guy Manning collaborated with me to provide the exquisite artwork for the cover and internal illustrations, and I am so grateful for his enthusiasm and patience, as well as being in awe of his remarkable talent. Olwen Fowler's skilled typesetting and design, an art of its own, has turned this book into a thing of beauty.

My dear friends Charlie and Charlotte read early drafts and gave valuable feedback. You are both so appreciated.

Thanks to Howard for so many lovely hours spent chatting while we watched our osprey, or waited for her, at the moorings. Those weeks will always be counted as the most special of my life.

Bianca and Pete, thank you for taking on wren duty when we had to go out, and for viewing the task as a pleasure and not a chore. You are such good friends. Thanks, too, to the wrens themselves for fledging their chicks a couple of days before our wedding, so that Si and I could go and get married without having to action Plan B (or simply refuse to leave the house, which was something I was seriously considering, should they still be in residence).

I'm truly able to be myself with you, Si, in all my obsessive weirdness. Thank you for always being so receptive when I talk at you about ospreys, fret about wrens, and invite you to join me at the window to admire the sparrows gossiping around the bird bath. I love you.

The biggest thanks, of course, must go to the animals themselves. They are one of the best things in my life.